A Handbook
on
Open-Air Evangelism

JP Earnest

Other Contributors:
Edwin Baker, Roger Carswell, Paul Linnell,
Andy Little, Mike Mellor & Sam Webster

© Day One Publications 2022

British Library Cataloguing in Publication Data available

ISBN 978-1-84625-720-9

Day One Publications
Ryelands Road, Leominster, HR6 8NZ, UK
Telephone 01568 613 740
North America Toll Free 888 329 6630
email sales@dayone.co.uk
web www.dayone.co.uk

Printed by 4edge Limited

Contents

Preface

Since the society's conception in 1853, The Open-Air Mission has sought to present the gospel of the Lord Jesus Christ to the masses in the public arena. Amongst its other aims and objectives, the Mission has also endeavoured to assist, nurture, train and develop others in open-air evangelism. By the grace of God, the work of OAM continues to this day—engaging non-Christians with the good news of Jesus and equipping Christians to share this good news.

It was back in the 1980s when staff Evangelist Edwin Baker and the then General Secretary, Alan Greenbank, compiled a helpful booklet for believers. Entitled *A Handbook on Open-Air Evangelism*, it has been a great help and encouragement to many down through the years. However, despite so many books on witnessing which have been produced since then, very little exists to practically encourage and nurture a biblical and winsome evangelism in the open-air.

This book seeks to build upon that 'how-to' guide developed by Edwin and Alan, drawing from much experience gained in the intervening years. Although primarily designed to help those engaged in open-air outreach (or indeed, interested in getting involved), there are numerous helpful hints and tips which will assist any believer in sharing their faith with others. The aim of this publication is to make a positive impact in nurturing and encouraging a God-honouring evangelism, especially in the open-air.

It is our prayer that this reference guide will be a help and a blessing to many, to the praise of God's glory. We also pray that we may see a revival of gospel outreach beyond the four walls of our churches, seeking to lovingly present Christ to the Christ-less masses.

Foreword

I well remember my first few faltering attempts at open-air preaching. The pounding heart, the dry mouth, the sense of being completely out of my comfort zone and then those few stumbling words trying to share the gospel with passers-by. How I wish I had been able to read this great little book before I started!

This book is written by men from the coalface, who have been out there, year in and year out, summer and winter. They know what they are talking about; and it is not surprising therefore that this book is full of helpful advice and wise counsel for those already involved in open air work or thinking of venturing out for the first time. Actually, it is also full of advice that needs to be taken on board in every form of evangelism.

I have seen these men in action on the streets. What has impressed me, as much as the clarity of the gospel they have preached, is the wise and winsome way in which they have done so. What a difference a smiling face can make as you preach! How important it is to make the main things the main things. This book is full of common sense and practical advice. Of course, getting the gospel right is central, but thinking about how you come across and where you set up your board and what your visual aids look like matter more than you think; and this book helps to think through those matters too. Just as important as the men preaching are those faithful men and women who come and stand and support; forming a crowd, giving out tracts, following up those who have stopped and listened. The worth and importance of these people is recognised in this book, and there is helpful advice for you if that is your role in the work.

My prayer is that JP and others like him will see their prayers answered through this book, in seeing more Christians ready to head out onto the streets, and, more importantly, see people come to Christ through faithful, gracious, Spirit-filled preaching and communication of the wonderful gospel of Jesus.

Pastor Hugh Collier
Great Ellingham, Norfolk

1. The Priority

We all have our 'happy place', that location where we love to retreat to and rest. For myself, it is a quiet and secluded small cabin in the woods. In Luke 9, Jesus sends out His disciples to preach and to heal. It is in Mark 6 where we learn of the weary disciples returning to report back on all that they had said and done. Seeing how busy they had been, the Lord Jesus invites them to, 'Come aside by yourselves to a deserted place and rest a while' (Mark 6:31). Departing by boat across the Sea of Galilee, they set off for this quiet and desolate place. But seeing who it was in the ship, folk from the surrounding area ran ahead of them to wait for their arrival.

If my wife and I were to set out for our 'happy place' only to find it was as busy as Piccadilly Circus, I guess we would feel quite disappointed and disillusioned! What was the response of Jesus to being greeted by a vast crowd? 'And Jesus, when He came out, saw a great multitude and was moved with compassion for them' (Mark 6:34a). Why such a loving concern and pity for these people? '... because they were like sheep not having a Shepherd' (Mark 6:34b). So, the Good Shepherd Himself seeks to tend these sheep, 'So He began to teach them many things' (Mark 6:34c). On seeing the crowd, Christ was moved with compassion, but that compassion moved Him to action. Please note, His priority was to instruct them from the Word of God.

> On seeing the crowd, Christ was moved with compassion, but that compassion moved Him to action

I wonder how many of us would naturally look upon a crowd as a nuisance? Yet, the Lord showed great concern for these shepherd-less people. Perhaps we need to look again at the crowds and love them as the lost sheep that they are and seek to point them to the Good Shepherd who lays down His life for the sheep? If we are not concerned for the lost, then we will never look for ways to reach out to them with the life-giving and life-saving message of the gospel.

Of all the ways in which the Lord has blessed the church to evangelise, surely the one method with the potential of reaching many, personally and directly, is open-air evangelism? Yes, we should always explore ways to promote the gospel in the life of the church—praise God for those opportunities! But let's face it, it is hard to encourage people to come to our gospel services or events. We rejoice when the unsaved actually darken the doorstep of the church, but in the experience of many churches that is rare. The open-air is a good starting point, that first contact with the gospel.

There have always been critics of taking the gospel onto the streets. In my experience, most critics, if they are honest, would say they had been put off open-air work because they had seen it done badly. Do we write off pulpit preaching on the Lord's Day because we've experienced some poor examples? Of course we don't. Though there have been poor, embarrassing and even shameful examples of evangelism outside, we should not dismiss everything on that basis.

Some have dismissed open-air work on the basis that the area is 'too hard'. If I had a penny for every time I had heard that said, I would be a very rich man! The truth is, every area is hard. Why? Because the hearts of the people are naturally hardened to the gospel. Any true openness to the truth of

God's Word is only seen because of the Holy Spirit's work. How we must pray for hard hearts, not just to be softened but graciously and sovereignly opened to receive Christ as Saviour and Lord!

Never believe anyone who tells you that open-air work is easy, because it is not! Read the diaries of John Wesley and you will see he always found it difficult. A well-seasoned preacher was once asked, 'Do you still get butterflies in your stomach every time you preach?' The experienced preacher responded, 'Yes, but they have learnt to fly in formation!' To reach out with the gospel of Christ in an ever-increasingly secular society is counter-cultural and therefore hard. Christians will 'stick out like sore thumbs' and will be the subject of many a joke. But we remember, 'The message of the cross is foolishness to those who are perishing, but to us who are being saved it is the power of God' (1 Corinthians 1:18). So much so that Paul could say to the Romans, 'I am not ashamed of the gospel of Christ, for it is the power of God to salvation for everyone who believes…' (Romans 1:16a). The fear of man will keep us from vital gospel proclamation, but a loving concern for the lost will motivate us to point them to Jesus Christ.

> The fear of man will keep us from vital gospel proclamation, but a loving concern for the lost will motivate us to point them to Jesus Christ

The 'Great Commission', as it is known, is to 'Go into all the world and preach the gospel to every creature' (Mark 16:15). Open-air work certainly reaches more than would ever hear inside. Wesley said that he knew of no other method of preaching the gospel to every creature. Jesus said 'Go', but so often, if we are honest, we are slow. More often excuses rather than reasons hinder us. We may not all be called to preach in the open-air but there is certainly a role for every believer. As the old hymn says, 'There's a work for Jesus none but you can do!' Let us take every opportunity the Lord gives us corporately as a church and individually as believers, but let us not neglect the tried and tested method of open-air work.

May the Lord grant us a greater love for the lost and help us in our weakness, so that we might seek to declare God's Word winsomely on the streets of our nation. And, as we work, we pray that He might work by His Spirit, causing the good seed of the gospel to fall on good soil to bring forth a plenteous harvest for His glory and His alone.

2. The Pattern

Gospel proclamation out-of-doors has been a blessed work down through the years and God's blessing continues to be seen today. Preaching has always been fundamental to open-air evangelism. We have examples of such open-air preaching in Scripture, for example Ezra and the Levites publicly reading and explaining God's Word in the public square (not the temple courts which would have precluded some); The Apostle Paul in Athens – not just with the Areopagus (an established and organised meeting place) but daily in the market place 'with those who happened to be there' (Acts 17:17b). Where did Peter preach on the Day of Pentecost? Where did Jonah preach the impending judgment of God? Though the Bible does not use the words, 'in the open-air', it is obvious that these men, and more besides, preached in the open-air!

Examples of bold open-air preaching are not just confined to the pages of Scripture, they have continued throughout church history. For example, John Wycliffe and the Lollards in the 14th Century, George Whitefield and John Wesley in the 18th Century, to name but a few. J.C. Ryle described the open-air work of the latter as 'the agency that transformed a nation'. Commenting on their practice Ryle wrote, 'If the pulpit of a parish was open to them, they gladly availed themselves of it. If it could not be obtained, they were

> **Examples of bold open-air preaching are not just confined to the pages of Scripture, they have continued throughout church history**

equally ready to preach in a barn. No place came amiss to them. In the field or by the road-side, on the village-green or in a market-place, in lanes or in alleys, in cellars or in garrets, on a tub or on a table, on a bench or on a horse-block, wherever hearers could be gathered, the spiritual reformers of the eighteenth century were read to speak to them about their souls ... Can we wonder that it produced a great effect?'

The 19th Century Baptist preacher, Charles Haddon Spurgeon, was also a strong advocate of open-air work. Not only was he himself an open-air preacher, he would instruct his trainee ministers on the art and the necessity of open-air preaching. There are two of his seminars on open-air preaching recorded in 'Lectures to my Students'—well worth a read. Addressing the ministerial sceptic, Mr Spurgeon said, 'No sort of defence is needed for preaching out of doors; but it would need very potent arguments to prove that a man had done his duty who has never preached beyond the walls of his meeting-house' (Lecture 18, *Open-Air Preaching* – Remarks Thereon). For these reasons, Spurgeon felt an affinity with the work of The Open-Air Mission.

More contemporary examples of God's working out-of-doors can be seen in the regular work of The Open-Air Mission and similar organisations. Evangelists and associate workers are regularly engaging passers-by with the gospel through a winsome public proclamation in preaching, distributing gospel literature and one-to-one conversations. Reports from the workers testify to many showing an openness to the gospel and being helped to understand the responsibility to repent and believe the good news. In our apathetic times, it is truly remarkable and encouraging to see the Lord at work in this way. There are often those who have also attended church to hear more having been referred to a Bible-believing, gospel-preaching local church. (As I write this, someone came to our church yesterday as a result of being contacted on the street.) Then, not as often as we would like, there are reports of those who have come to saving faith in Jesus Christ having first heard the gospel explained in the open-air.

The primacy of preaching is seen in these examples, but sadly preaching is often looked upon negatively today (and not just by the unbelieving world). We cannot expect the unregenerate to appreciate God's Word when it is alien to them without the sovereign work of the Holy Spirit. It ought to be saddening for believers to see a downgrading of preaching—not just in the pulpit but also on the pavement.

Preaching is not to be reduced to a few 'blessed thoughts', neither should slogans and 'one-liners' like, 'Don't be a sinner, be a winner!' be mistaken as preaching. Real preaching is to faithfully proclaim the truth and meaning of the Bible whilst applying its relevance to those in front of us.

> **Real preaching is to faithfully proclaim the truth and meaning of the Bible whilst applying its relevance to those in front of us**

When preaching is downgraded, certain topics are ignored or neglected. Preaching about sin, death and Hell is often viewed as something that would 'put people off'; but set in its correct gospel-context it is vital we convey such truths. Preaching must be balanced—first the bad news so that the good news is appreciated as good news.

Of course, the balance can often be wrong. Christianity is often characterised by pendulum-swing reactions from one extreme to another. The open-air preacher who often attracts negative publicity is most often (though not exclusively) one who hones in on particular sins. All sin is an offence to a holy God and so we must present sin in that balanced way. Some preachers can fall into the trap of 'denouncing rather than announcing'—denouncing particular sins rather than announcing the Saviour of sinners!

To the church at Colosse, Paul gave some helpful advice: 'Let your speech always be with grace, seasoned with salt' (Colossians 4:6a). The congregation at the synagogue of Nazareth 'marvelled at the gracious words which proceeded out of His mouth' (Luke 4:22b). As ever, our Lord Jesus is a great example to us. Grace should characterise our communication of the gospel. However, we must also ensure our presentation of the gospel is 'salted'. Salt to flavour food is often frowned upon today, but one of its main uses back then was as a preservative. Long before refrigeration, meat and fish would be kept from 'going bad' by using salt. It prevented the food spoiling or corrupting. Seasoning our speech with salt is to ensure there is nothing bad in our preaching or conversation—nothing which could spoil, nothing which corrupts.

However, to faithfully share the gospel we cannot just dwell on the fact that 'God is love'. If the gospel was only about a loving God, people could legitimately say, 'So what?' and dismiss any claims the message has upon them. To faithfully proclaim the gospel, we must also be prepared to declare that 'God is just'—a God who holds sinners accountable. Just as salt is sharp and bitter to the taste, biblical themes such as sin, death and Hell will also be sharp and bitter to non-Christians. That is why, according to Paul, we need to ensure gracious communication, seasoned with salt. How easy it is to get the balance wrong—erring to one side rather than faithfully presenting both the love of God and the justice of God. In his commentary on Colossians, Guy Appéré makes this helpful point: 'The gentleness of grace should not make the salt lose its sharpness, nor should the sharpness of salt take away the gentleness of grace. Salt and grace should not neutralise but strengthen each other' (*The Mystery of Christ*).

There are many components to an open-air meeting (see chapter 7) but, where appropriate, the greatest weapon in our gospel arsenal is preaching (which is why a whole chapter is given over to the subject in this handbook). Many of the blessings of yesteryear were through the faithful, public heralding of the good news. Open-air preaching was often at the heart of awakenings and revivals. Let us learn from the pattern of biblical and church history. May we not be guilty of downgrading gospel proclamation (inside or outside) but ever seek to nurture and cultivate that biblical and winsome approach to better engage with non-Christians. Praise God for the freedom we have to speak and express our faith in the public arena. Whilst we enjoy this liberty and pray for its continuation, let us seek to avail ourselves of this God-given opportunity.

> Open-air preaching was often at the heart of awakenings and revivals

3. The Place

'We fish where the fish are'. In other words, we go where the people are. It would not be wise to deploy our limited resources in quieter places. Surely, we want to concentrate on reaching as many as possible?

In the history of The Open-Air Mission, evangelists would preach at racecourses, fairgrounds, factory gates and even at public executions! Things have changed over the years. No longer are there crowds to address at lunch hour outside a factory or at a public hanging attracting spectators. Even some racecourses and fairgrounds are no longer open to us as opportunities because they operate on private land. So where are crowds generally found today?

Where to go?

In our consumer-driven age, most people gravitate towards shops, salons and snack bars. Mike Mellor has much experience of open-air work and has contributed the helpful chapter on preaching (see chapter 4). It is on the pedestrianised streets of our towns and cities that, as Mike says, 'The Lord has literally paved the way for us to preach the gospel.' High streets with their banks, cafés and shops generally bring good footfall and are away from most traffic noise. Sometimes where no pedestrianised zone exists, a wide pavement area suffices. So, let us think practically about the public place as the best venue for an open-air witness.

Where to stand?

Police and local authority workers would naturally raise an objection if we were blocking the highway or interfering with the trade of vendors nearby. We need to be wise in where we operate. Before you set up, have a look around.

- **Is this public or private property?** If the street is owned by a private company then you cannot operate there without permission.

- **Is this the best place to stand?** We want to maximise the opportunity and stand where there is good footfall and minimal distractions—perhaps even somewhere near benches where people can sit and listen?

- **Is there a busker nearby?** Then you probably want to be far away from them!

- **Am I too near a shop doorway or a street vendor?** We do not want to hinder their trade and cause animosity when we are trying to present the gospel of peace!

- **Am I causing an obstruction?** Could an emergency or service vehicle pass safely down the road? Often, if using a display board or a table, positioning next to an existing obstruction (such as a lamppost) is the wisest place to stand.

When to go?

- **Is one day busier than another?** Sometimes Saturdays are the busiest day in a particular place. Or, perhaps there is a market on a certain day which brings increased footfall?

- **Is there a particular time of day that is more conducive to open-air work?** Is the lunchtime period busier as more people are out and about? Is there a college or university nearby which brings lots of students out after lectures mid to late afternoon? Some cosmopolitan places have evening opportunities with people out for a stroll or visiting bars and restaurants.

- **Is there a particular opportunity?** Sometimes one-off events in the town/city can provide additional opportunities. Is there an annual carnival or festival which would bring more onto the pedestrianised streets?

There is no 'one size fits all' approach. Every town and city is different, therefore that requires a prayerful wisdom as to when best to operate. Sometimes, 'trial and error' is the best way to learn.

It often comes as a surprise to people to learn that on pedestrianised shopping precincts we do not require permission to hold an open-air. The laws relating to freedom of speech and freedom of expression in the United Kingdom allow us to freely proclaim and express the gospel of the Lord Jesus Christ. Public highways (such as a pedestrianised high street) are open to gospel outreach. However, we must beware of straying onto private property – such as a privately-owned shopping centre (further help on this subject is given in chapter 10).

There are numerous tell-tale signs of a public highway— council bins and street furniture (often with the local authority's logo on it), street lamps, signage, paving etc. If these are consistent with everything else locally, you are on safe ground. But if these things are different from council property (sometimes benefiting from better investment) you are likely to be on private property. A careful look before you start an open-air could prevent any awkward situations arising!

Whilst assisting one of the OAM evangelists in an east Midlands town, a pedestrianised quadrangle seemed the best place to stand. Unfortunately, it seemed it was owned by the adjoining shopping centre and therefore private property. Yet, on closer inspection, there was a subtle difference in street furniture half way down. This indicated that fifty percent of it was, actually, public space. The evangelist suggested contacting the council to ask. However, in explaining my theory to him, I recommended a much easier approach. 'What we need to do is watch the council worker when he comes to empty the bins!' Sure enough, after a few minutes a man dressed in yellow came along pushing a dustcart and began emptying bins near us. Making small-talk about the weather I struck up a conversation. I asked, 'Do you have to empty those bins over there in the square?' to which he replied, 'Only to half way!' Theory proved, public land ascertained, and a better opportunity ensued. (By the way, I did leave the council worker with a gospel tract and thanked him for his help!)

Well-meaning Christians have often approached local authorities for permission which has been declined. Sometimes this has meant no outreach took place or the refusal being contested. Thankfully, we do not generally need to ask permission. If we do, we run the risk of giving them licence to say 'no'. However, we are not reckless and local authorities and their third-parties can raise legitimate concerns about safety etc. These things are covered in chapter 10.

4. The Preacher

Whilst we may not agree with all of his theology, Dr Anthony Thorold (Bishop of Rochester 1877–1891 and Bishop of Winchester 1891–1895) gave this helpful advice:

'To be listened to is the first thing, *therefore be interesting*.
To be understood is the second, *therefore be clear*.
To be useful is the third, *so be practical*.
To be obeyed is the fourth, *so speak with authority*.'

In this chapter, experienced evangelist Mike Mellor looks at:

The Man—*Who should preach?*
The Message—*What should be preached?*
The Manner—*How should it be preached?*

The Man: *Who should preach?*

No-one should be put off from considering preaching in the open-air. Many a pastor and evangelist were 'launched' by stuttering a few incoherent sentences in an open air setting. However, it is vital that to preach on a regular basis, certain gifts should be evident in the man. There are necessary qualities which have developed given time and opportunity. If you are unsure that you possess the necessary gifting for this work, ask a mature and experienced leader or team member or two to give you their honest assessment—'Faithful are the wounds of a friend'! (Proverbs 27:6a).

The qualifications for an open-air preacher were published by The Open-Air Mission and quoted by C. H. Spurgeon to his students many years ago. These still provide a good outline for what we should be aiming for:

- A good voice.

- Naturalness of manner.

- Self-possession.

- A good knowledge of Scripture and of everyday things.

- Ability to adapt himself to any audience.

- Good illustrative powers.

- Zeal, prudence, and common sense.

- A large, loving heart.

- Sincere belief in all he says.

- Entire dependence on the Holy Spirit for success.

- A close walk with God by prayer.

- A consistent walk before men by a holy life.

Whatever subject you are preaching on, there must be life, fire, and energy in the man and total reliance upon the Holy Spirit. Be ever mindful of the words of Him who sent you, 'for without me you can do nothing' (John 15:5b).

The Message: *What should we preach?*

Much could be said about the content we preach, but let us strip it down to the essentials. Saints of old used to speak about 'the Three Rs' of preaching—*Ruin*, *Redemption* and *Regeneration*:

Ruin (Genesis 3:14–15; Romans 3:23)

When we speak to our post-Christian generation about Jesus coming to save us, their minds automatically think, 'Saved from what?' So, we must explain how mankind is in rebellion against its Maker, has broken His law, and how the whole world is under God's curse not His blessing. As a result, every human being now lives under the shadow of God's just wrath and will endure it for all eternity. We can then follow up with the 'But…'—even in that first book of the Bible there is a promise of One who will come on a rescue mission to bring hope.

Redemption (2 Corinthians 5:21; 1 Corinthians 2:2)

This is the good news that transcends the bad news—God Himself in the person of the Lord Jesus Christ has entered into our world as a Saviour. The preaching of the cross of Christ is indispensable and is at the very heart of our message. We must stress that only by personal repentance and faith in the substitutionary death of Jesus Christ upon the cross can a person's sin be forgiven. The power is always in the cross and the truth that the Holy Spirit delights to honour—even though it is 'foolishness to those who are perishing' (1 Corinthians 1:18b) And let us not forget to preach the resurrection!

Regeneration (John 3:3–8; 2 Corinthians 5:17)

Every conversion is a miracle, and it is the miracle of the 'new birth' that we pray for every time we preach. Unless a person is born again (born from above) they will not enter Heaven. It is God who opens blind eyes, unstops deaf ears and raises the dead—and He can do it. But we must not neglect to preach regeneration, how the Holy Spirit can transform the vilest sinner into the most beautiful saint. This is the wonder of the gospel we preach!

These then, are the bare bones of the gospel. Of course, it is our duty to 'flesh out' and clothe them as attractively and enticingly as possible. But our message will not stand without this vital skeleton. So, in your mind go through the checklist every time you preach so that however attractive the 'clothes' of your message might be (and must be!), let us ensure 'the Three Rs' are in there.

Connecting in a way that produces repentance

We seek to be faithful in our preaching of the gospel and desire to hold nothing back of the seriousness of sin. Like the Apostle Paul, we want to preach 'repentance toward God and faith toward our Lord Jesus Christ' (Acts 20:21). However, we can do this in a way that is theologically sound but mechanical and fails to reach the heart of our hearers in a way that produces change. The danger then is that we are satisfied we have faithfully preached the gospel because we have presented the right 'formulas'. For example:

You + sin = Hell
Repent + believe = Heaven

We might presume that an angry response to our message is conviction of sin. But often it is a fleshly response rather than a Spirit-wrought conviction. It is important we regularly search ourselves, examining both presentation and manner in our preaching to see where we can improve and be more effective.

Approaching his adulterous and deceitful king, the prophet Nathan does not set out to just deliver the bare truth, 'You have committed adultery, murdered and lied! You have broken the commandments. Repent!' No, he wants his message to reach the very depths of David's heart in order to ensure that 'godly sorrow produces repentance' (2 Corinthians 7:10). So, he skilfully unfolds (to a former shepherd!) a heartbreaking story of a rich man who cruelly steals a poor man's only possession, 'a little ewe lamb'. Burning with anger, David rages that this man deserves to die. Nathan has his congregation 'on the ropes', so now comes in with 'the killer blow'... 'You are the man!' (2 Samuel 12:7a). Boom! Truth, wisely communicated in the power of the Holy Spirit. Preaching that connected. Undoubtedly, we have hard things to set before people at times—sin, judgment, everlasting punishment. But how to most effectively communicate these vital subjects is a matter for us to continually wrestle with in our ministries.

The Manner: *How should we preach?*

Most, if not all preachers will have a grasp of what must be preached, but we come now to an area which I feel needs the most attention—the manner in which we communicate these eternal truths to a generation which not only is in such spiritual ignorance, but has so little an appetite for spiritual things.

1. Preacher's credibility

The preacher's initial aim is to connect with his hearers. The challenge is first to gain their attention before even attempting to address their hearts and minds. This is challenging enough in a pulpit over a period of thirty to forty minutes, but it takes twice the effort to achieve in a street setting, where we are not known and have no credibility or point of reference whatsoever. We convey the gospel in words, but by much more than words. From the very start, there must be an awareness that even before a word is heard, people will look at us and make judgments. We cannot afford to be self-conscious, but we do need to be self-aware and give a thought to how we must appear to the unsuspecting public, who will see this strange spectacle of open-air preaching when passing by on their way shopping, going for meal or whatever. People must be able to take one look at us, even from a distance and think, 'I don't know what that guy's saying, but he seems a pretty sane, normal, reasonable person.' We aim to arouse curiosity, but in a positive way!

2. Hook

All preachers, whether inside or outside a church need a 'hook' when opening their message. That is, right from the start of our message, hearers will say inwardly, 'I'm interested in this. There is something here for me.' But in open-air work, it is so much harder as we have no waiting audience—they have their minds set on anything and everything but listening to a 'religious sermon'! But you are part of that 'hook' and we have just seconds to convince people we have something to say of interest and relevance. And importantly, we need to look as though we ourselves have been affected by this same good news! As C.H. Spurgeon said, 'There are many more flies caught with honey than with vinegar and there are many more sinners brought to Christ by happy Christians than by doleful Christians!' (C.H. Spurgeon, Sermon 2405: *Joy, a Duty*; preached Metropolitan Tabernacle, 24th March 1895).

In these days of such spiritual apathy, it is a tremendous challenge simply getting people to stop and consider our vital message. Throwing out questions can be one way arresting passers-by. It is significant to note that beside using captivating stories and imagery, Jesus would ask probing questions. We could, for example, seek to introduce the problem of sin in the human heart (especially if on the display board you have some of the 'symptoms' of our heart-problem: war, greed, stabbings, abuse, murder etc.) by asking a group of young people as they pass: 'Hey, what is wrong with us? Why is it, after all these years, we still can't love each other?' (There is an opening there also into the subject of evolution.) Let us use all legitimate means to engage with people, trying to stop them in their tracks and so hear a presentation of the gospel.

Finally, bear in mind that many will not have been present for the start of our message, so there should be a repetitive, recapping, cyclical approach to our method, yet always with freshness.

3. Dress
We don't want to be pernickety here, but how we look does matter. We want to blend into our particular setting rather than unhelpfully stand out. First impressions can either help or hinder the preacher and our message. Let us avoid the 'weirdometer' registering any more than it ought!

4. Speech and language
To be sure, the dynamics of public preaching are different from a conversational one-to-one setting, but we must beware of creating an unnecessary gulf between us.

- **Avoid a declaiming style**
  Some street preachers say they are preaching in love but can come over as quite hostile. The tone of our voice is of great importance. Also, we can have the right message, but the wrong attitude. 'We are not Old Testament prophets', says Roger Carswell in his book, *Evangelistic Living*. We must make the gospel sound like the good news that it is.

26

- **Be aware**

  Be especially aware of those occasions when having to compete with surrounding noise (traffic, buskers etc.) as very often the louder we try to speak, the more our faces are likely to contort, giving off an angry look, even if we are not angry. The louder we speak, the harsher we may sound. There is a difference between shouting and projecting one's voice naturally.

  > **TIPS**
  > - Beware of your 'off days'! (Disagreement with spouse, problems parking the car etc.)
  > - Be careful on those days when there is little response—apart from comments made that undermine your confidence and have made you feel defensive and vulnerable!
  > - Remember—in rejecting us, people are not necessarily rejecting Christ.

- **Be natural**

  Both in you personally and in your preaching, be natural. It is helpful for the preacher to think to himself, 'How would I speak if my unconverted cousin, mum or mate at work was passing by? What tone of voice would I use?'

- **Language**

  The words we use must be jargon-free ... and intelligible. *We* know what we mean by 'sin', 'salvation', 'eternal life', but what does that mean to a pagan Brit? Simple Anglo-Saxon English, spoken clearly and at a good pace is not only helpful for British folk but is essential for non-native English speakers in our communities.

- **Tone of voice**

  Our tone must be attractive. No ranting or screaming. John Wesley was quick to condemn loud preaching, or 'screaming' as he called it. He writes to one of his men, 'Scream no more, at the peril of your soul … Speak with all your heart, but with a moderate voice.' To another he wrote, 'Never scream. Never speak above the natural pitch of your voice; it is disgustful to the hearers…'. As JP Earnest often says, 'I prefer to preach *to* people, not *at* people'. There is a big difference between throwing a ball *to* someone and *at* them!

TIPS

Be wise in the choice of location.
AVOID:

- Too narrow a street—your voice may sound extra loud and intrusive.

- Too wide a space where there is nothing to use as a sounding board for your voice.

- Speaking as though addressing the whole city ("Good afternoon Birmingham!"), but speak as if addressing just one person.

- Use of amplification if possible. The aim is to draw people to us, not keep them at a distance.

- Setting up near vendors, buskers (or anyone whose income could be affected). Choose somewhere where you are not likely to cause an obstruction and therefore be 'moved on'.

Helpful book:

Mike Mellor, *Look after your voice: Taking care of the preacher's greatest asset* (Day One Publications)

5. Eye contact

Speak as though addressing one person and try to make a point of looking at people in their eyes. Not staring, but warm, natural eye-contact. Think as you preach, 'She could be my gran,' 'He could be my wayward brother,' 'She could be my rebellious niece,' or 'That furrow-browed businessman could be about to take his life,' etc. People should be able to detect we have a genuine concern for them and eye contact can help draw people in to listen further.

6. Hecklers

Good hecklers are worth their weight in gold and can be a great means in helping to draw a crowd. But we need to handle them with great grace and wisdom. However, if the heckler is one who gives no opportunity for you to speak, then terminate the conversation (not the heckler!) Be sure to be gracious and polite at all times, your response is being closely examined at such times. Very often we fail to win the heckler but gain the sympathy and interest of those who stopped to see the 'action'. At all times, we must seek to win our hearers with a 'cocktail' of love and logic. Onlookers closely observe in a pressure situation not just what we say but how we say it in our response to a heckler.

7. Remember the source of power—the cross of our Lord Jesus Christ!

Let us learn from the apostle Paul's great conviction, 'I determined not to know anything among you except Jesus Christ and Him crucified' (1 Corinthians 2:2). When we have done our best to present our best arguments and to be as appealing as we can, we are praying for a miracle from Heaven to convict of sin, open blind eyes, unstop deaf ears and convert hearts of stone to flesh. Only God can make dead people live, and although the preaching of the cross is 'foolishness to those who are perishing' (1 Corinthians 1:18) it is at the heart of God's saving work and the Holy Spirit uniquely honours the preaching of Christ crucified ... and risen! Never forget to preach the resurrection.

8. Know when to end the message

I've seen men with a good crowd, and thought at a certain point, 'This would be the time to close' (i.e. urge them to repent and trust Christ, offer a Gospel of John or other literature etc.), but the preacher goes on ... and on ... and on ... and the crowd drifts away. Opportunity lost.

5. The Presentation

Following on from the chapter on preaching, some thought should be given as to how we present our message in the open-air. A display board is a useful tool in the open-air, whether it be a bespoke design or just a whiteboard and an easel, it can add something to our presence. Not only does it 'anchor' the preacher, preventing them from roaming, it also provides a focal point meaning they aren't just a random voice heard and not easily identified. Here is someone who is serious about what they are saying and is determined to convey it audibly and visually.

Have you ever seen a newscaster present a TV news bulletin? First, there are the headlines to grab your attention at the very start. Then follows the explanation coupled with helpful visuals on screen to maintain your interest. A short conclusion normally 'wraps up' the item without 'dragging it on'. News programmes are often fast paced to convey facts whilst trying to ensure every viewer watches until the end of the show.

Such news bulletins are full of bad news, but we as gospel preachers have good news for the people! What we convey is of more vital importance and so we must give careful consideration as to how we present this good news. We need a 'headline' (or a 'hook' as Mike calls in it the previous chapter) to grab the attention of those passing by. Once we have stirred the interest of passers-by, we give the explanation of what we have to say—clearly and concisely. Maintaining interest is difficult just by words alone and so we can help convey our message with visual aids. But 'aids' are all that they are, something visual to aid the verbal message. The moment visuals take over and become more prominent, they cease to be 'aids' and become gimmicks. We must draw to a close at an appropriate time and so we need to be mindful of attention spans, seeking to apply the gospel to those listening in conclusion. Offering helpful literature and being available to talk further should be the last word.

So, let's think through some of the components of our presentation in detail:

The 'headline' or 'hook'

The title of our message could be a statement or a question. Something topical or something spiritual. Questions are more often than not helpful because they invite a response (if not outwardly, then inwardly). But we must not fall into the trap of trying to answer questions that nobody is asking! Our questions must be relevant if they are to work as a 'hook' to 'reel people in' to listen to our gospel presentation. Such 'hooks' will be drawn from Scripture or gospel controversies. We can also draw from topical news and current affairs or even a particular contemporary or historical event relevant to that place.

Think back to a news bulletin you have seen on TV or a newspaper cover you have glanced at—how did they try to grab your attention? It is always something short and to the point. But our inspiration for the substance of the title will not be found in a tabloid newspaper. It will be found in the gospel material we want to convey. For example, if we are burdened to speak on the reality and implications of the resurrection, then we might choose a title such as: *Jesus Christ—Dead or Alive?* If we are burdened to speak on eternal life through trusting Jesus, we might go for: *Life, Death … what next?* If our topic is the exclusivity of Christ then a question we could use is: *Why is Jesus the only way to God?* As we think through what we want to share in our message, those ideas will be the source of inspiration for a natural but catchy 'hook'.

Whatever we settle on, our title should be clearly and prominently displayed and declared as we begin our presentation. The late Frank Cockrem, General Secretary of The Open-Air Mission, gave this advice in his *Handbook to Highway Witnessing*, in the first decade of the last century: 'The style of an open-air address should be, as far as possible, the very opposite of sermonic and ministerial. Instead of commencing with a formal announcement of a text, it should aim to captivate the hearers' attention in the first sentence or two by an utterance at once informal, sympathetic, and illustrative; thus predisposing the listener to attend while the heart of the subject is reached. This needs careful thought, and the introduction of an address should be well studied beforehand, whenever possible, for it will usually decide the success or failure of the whole effort.'

Content

Our headline may be both eye- and ear-catching, but the content of our message is fundamental. Once we have grabbed the mind of a passer-by, we must inform that mind whilst ultimately aiming for their hearts. We will employ logic and reason, backed-up with the authority of God's Word. We need to be careful not just to become a machine gun, firing Bible verses at people— verses coupled by a connection *we* see but our hearers do not. Simply state the fact, illustrate it to help understanding, apply it to them personally and back it up with Scripture. The preacher then should be disciplined to think through his presentation.

How easy it is to get off topic or to get 'bogged down' in detail or jargon. Our message shouldn't be something we ramble through incoherently, there should be a structure to it. It is often joked that a good sermon always has three points—that is not a bad pattern to follow, inside or outside. Three simple points are memorable and thought-provoking, bringing structure and stability to a message. The preacher should be disciplined to have prepared an outline beforehand.

Visual aids don't just aid those we are reaching, they also help the preacher. If we have produced captions and illustrations for each sermon point, then, as we explain each of those points, we can add the relevant visuals to our display board. This helps maintain interest to those who may have stopped to listen. They can see that you are developing something. They can see the structure to your message. Plus, it has the added advantage of helping those who have stopped understand part-way through your talk, who you are and what you are saying. Visual aids, then, become our sermon notes. We would not be very engaging if we were just reading verbatim from a sheet of A4. Rather, developing our talk with visualised captions, these become our prompters and help keep

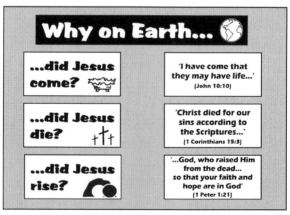

Example of a visualised talk

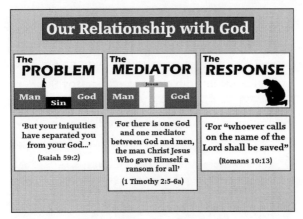

Example of a visualised talk

the preacher on track! It also frees up our eyes to have eye contact with people we are addressing, helping to draw them in to listen.

Some preachers say they like to preach from a text because they have great liberty in doing so—after all, they say, Whitefield never used illustrated talks on a display board! Preaching through a text is often very appropriate, but let us not get lazy and avoid some disciplined preparation. Anyone can slap a poster text on a board and then start on a discourse which is difficult for hearers to follow. Sometimes (and I have learnt from experience here) such a method drags out the message and is far less engaging. I used to get very frustrated when watching a weather forecast on TV. Sometimes the presenter would stand in front of the map and waffle on with very little reference to what was on display behind him. Guess what? I get very frustrated when preachers do the same!

If we are to preach from a text, let us give some serious thought to how best to present that. Give it a title. If it's a poster, cut it into pieces that you can add as you work your way through the verse. For example, when I have preached from 1 Timothy 2:5-6a in the open-air, I have printed it on six captions (each with an accompanying picture) and I have explained each one as I develop the text-based talk.

With just a little thought, a text has been turned into a more visually-enticing and engaging board talk.

Example of a visualised text

Conclusion

Once we have developed the main theme of our message, tying all the threads together, we move to the challenge and call of the gospel. What must they do in response to what they have heard? This too can be an illustrated caption and added as the 'pièce de résistance' as we draw to a close. Applying the gospel personally at the end is not a licence to repeat the whole sermon, rather it is the opportunity to briefly recap and remind, before emphasising repentance and faith. But be sure to offer something helpful hearers can take away with them. This could be a Gospel of John or other Christian literature, but make sure it has a point of contact to enable follow-up should they desire to know more.

Don't get 'bogged down' in your conclusion. Sometimes preachers can be like aeroplanes circling an airport in bad weather, unable to land. Bring the plane down swiftly and smoothly! 'Brevity, brevity and again brevity is a lesson I would most earnestly impress on every open-air worker for God,' said Frank Cockrem. John Wesley knew when to conclude a message and gave this advice: 'Better leave them longing than loathing!' In other words, 'leave them wanting more'—which could lead to further opportunities. Having these things in mind when preparing and delivering our message will be invaluable.

We want to be seen to be approachable and available as we close. If interest has been stirred, then we want them to feel they can take literature, ask questions and chat with us. But leave your visuals on display as long as possible. These will continue to preach after you have finished, conveying a reasoned and structured argument for the gospel.

Display boards

A display board is just that, an apparatus in order to display—but display what? Firstly, it can display whom we represent as believers locally (whether that be a church or an organisation). Helpful signage can identify us as being Christians as opposed to Jehovah's Witnesses or Latter-Day Saints etc. Some display boards (as commonly used by The Open-Air Mission) can also make gospel literature available for passers-by

to browse and freely take. Display boards can display the message being preached—not just targeting 'ear-gate' but 'eye-gate' to draw people in to listen. After all, 'The hearing ear and the seeing eye, the LORD has made them both' (Proverbs 20:12).

There are other soft benefits from using a board. It can prevent the preacher wandering around on the street and making it harder for people to listen. A display board can give the impression of something more 'professional' than spontaneous or 'ad-hoc'. Standing next to something which identifies us can give the impression of belonging and being accountable to a body—credibility which could give greater confidence to passers-by to stop and listen.

The best display boards are lightweight but sturdy enough to use safely. These can be easily transported and lashed to prevent the wind carrying them over. You may wish to consider making your own board or sourcing a flip-chart board, an artist's easel and board etc. Whatever you use, it needs to serve the purpose and not become a safety problem (see chapter 10). Detailed plans for constructing an OAM-style display board can be obtained from The Open-Air Mission.

TIP

Remember, the board is displaying Scripture texts and captions for the benefit of those you are trying to reach. With that in mind, address your audience—not the board! By all means gesture or point towards your displayed visuals, but don't talk to them! Many a preacher unwittingly looks at the board which means that their face and voice is no longer projected towards their hearers but away from them!

Visual aids

We have spoken much of the benefit of visual aids, and much of this has been developed through experience. The Open-Air Mission has been using visual aids for many years. Historically, a fabric banner would be held up beside the preacher, identifying the witness whilst displaying a verse of Scripture. However, the first recorded use of a visual aid was in the early 1870s by the then General Secretary, Gawin Kirkham. He had imported the now-famous painting, *The*

Gawin Kirkham's Broad and Narrow Way visual aid
© Peter N Millward. Used by kind permission

Broad and the Narrow Way, and had it translated and reproduced. Three canvas versions were commissioned, the last one being the largest, 9 feet by 12 feet, and displayed using an apparatus specially designed for the purpose. In low light, five duplex oil lamps illuminated the illustration as Gawin preached. Each relevant section was pointed out using a cane either by himself or sometimes by an assistant. Over a 30-year period, this was used over 1,000 times, reaching tens of thousands with the gospel.

These days, workers with OAM tend to use visualised talks (as described earlier in this chapter). Some examples of these talks can be freely downloaded from The Open-Air Mission website. Have a look through them. Even if you don't feel that 'glove' will fit your hand, get some ideas from them for you to develop your own. There is sometimes a place for an 'object lesson' as part of your message—as in something you hold in your hand. However, be aware that this has its limitations and so you may wish to use it as a visual aid to your visual aids!

The best visual aid I believe any preacher should use is their Bible. I am a firm believer in holding a Bible as a statement when I preach. I like a Bible handy so that I can refer to it in conversation, but I also like to hold a Bible as I preach—and a Bible that looks like a Bible! God's Word is our final authority and even just holding it as we preach can illustrate we are 'people of the book'.

But in terms of printed and laminated captions, preachers will inevitably vary in style and preference. However, one thing we should be agreed on is the principle of conveying truth as clearly as possible. Here are some questions to think through:

- **What sort of paper am I going to use?** White or coloured etc.?

- **Which font am I going to use?** We need something that is easily read and not a distraction.

- **What size of font will I use?** We don't want our visuals to turn into an eye test with people having to squint their eyes to try and read something!

- **Does using bold or italic typefaces emphasise or differentiate certain parts?** For example, titles or verses of Scripture.

- **Are there appropriate pictures I can use to help convey something?** Pictures that are not so complex that they require more staring than a 'Where's Wally?' picture! Clear clip-art images or good pictures that illustrate easily are the best. Beware of using copyrighted pictures.

- **Is less more?** Am I trying to put too much on display that it becomes a distraction?

- **How will I preserve and enhance my visuals?** Will I laminate them with a non-reflective matt or a glossy covering? How will I ensure no water ingress will spoil them by causing ink to smudge etc.?

- **How will I stick each caption to the display board?** Magnetic tape or 'Velcro' are often the best ways.

- **How will I keep them in order?** There's nothing worse (for the preacher or those listening!) than starting to preach and finding your captions are out-of-sync!

Well thought-through, well-designed, well-produced visuals are well-preserved. Put in the time and effort and they will be at your disposal in many an open-air in the future.

We would frown upon a preacher standing in a pulpit without having thoroughly and prayerfully prepared his material. May it not be so in the open-air! May we only dare to stand up and preach if we have given careful and prayerful consideration to our presentation so that it is the best it can be, for God's glory!

TIP

Always have something displayed on the board. Whether it be a Bible verse or a simple visualised talk, the board will continue to preach even if no-one is preaching!

---

6. The Personal Worker

Someone has stopped to listen—great. Someone has accepted a piece of literature—wonderful! What next? Personal work is the first and obvious follow-up. In gentle, open, eyeball to eyeball conversation we can take the enquirer deeper and more personally into the gospel.

It is often easier to strike up a conversation with a stranger in the open-air once they have shown an interest in some way. Notice I say 'conversation'. Dialogue is a two-way street. Beware of a monologue! They are not 'cannon fodder' lined up to have Bible verses fired at them. In gently chatting with the person we can find out more about them and then tailor our response to their particular situation or need. Someone once said, 'We have two ears and one mouth—so we must listen twice as much as we speak!'

As conversations deepen and develop, we need to exercise wisdom—when to stop! I've stopped myself, before now, saying too much in a conversation for fear of 'muddying the water' and distracting from the main focus of the conversation. Wisdom is also needed in gauging the response of those we are talking to. They are not to be held prisoner—if their body language is showing signs of impatience or unease, then draw the conversation to a close.

I can remember having to gently intervene in a conversation when the person clearly wanted to get away, but the Christian just wasn't reading the signs! I can also remember a well-meaning Christian holding on to the person, preventing them from leaving. There's a place for a direct challenge but it is better that people leave having heard a short explanation of the gospel in a pleasant manner, than to hastily leave feeling 'cornered' or 'button-holed'.

The moment we apply pressure in a conversation, we run the risk of alienating that individual. There is certainly merit in posing a challenge based on what they have heard, but pushing too hard could draw the conversation to an abrupt end.

I have had the joy of sitting with people in conversation who, in response to what they have heard, have expressed their desire to get right with God there and then. However, in most cases, I would rather send them on their way, knowing the gospel, taking something of the gospel (literature) and urging them to personally respond to the gospel in repentance and faith. This is the Lord's work and we must be careful not to manipulate people into making rash 'decisions'.

> **This is the Lord's work and we must be careful not to manipulate people**

I can remember one such conversation in Birmingham's city centre. A man had stopped to listen to the preacher and I was able to follow him up in conversation afterwards. He was open and receptive to the gospel and went on his way with a Gospel of John. Sadly, another Christian group were operating in the area and saw the man heading up the street and two of them engaged him in conversation. The body language of the man was very awkward and uncomfortable as these two Christians surrounded him. After a while, I ventured closer to see what was happening and heard the man say, 'Oh OK! OK! Yes, you can pray for me …' The two Christians laid hands on him and began praying—the man on the other hand, was like a 'rabbit caught in the headlights', looking around, very uncomfortable. After an 'Amen', the man bid a hasty retreat. Later, the two

Christians from this group approached me to boast that the man had asked Jesus into his heart! Undue pressure had not commended the gospel, but contradicted it. We are not playing the numbers game. We seek to point lost souls to Christ and let God do the inner work by His Spirit!

In this chapter, evangelist Roger Carswell seeks to help in the field of personal work:

One of the greatest joys in a Christian's life is that of speaking of the Lord Jesus to those who need to hear the most wonderful, yet urgent message in the world. Not every Christian is an evangelist, but every believer is a witness of Jesus their Lord and Saviour.

'The main thing is to keep the main thing the main thing' said D. L. Moody. We may have strong views on a multiplicity of issues, but let us follow the example of the Apostle Paul who said that he determined to know nothing other than Christ and Him crucified. Jesus, in commissioning His disciples, told them their fourfold message: His sufferings, His resurrection, the need for repentance, and the receiving of forgiveness. 'The Great Commission' is not discussing theology over a 'latte' or signing a petition to uphold Christian standards. It is good to be involved in kind, social deeds, but as Christians we know that what a person does with Jesus matters for eternity. In 100 years from now, everyone we know will be either in Heaven or in Hell. Personal evangelism is eternal work. It is clear that what everyone needs to hear is that, though we have sinned, there is a great Saviour and a freely-offered way of salvation. As an old chorus put it, 'Every person in every nation, in each succeeding generation, has the right to hear the news that Christ can save.'

I have always found that Jesus is strangely attractive and to speak of Him makes an immediate impact. Nowhere is this more clearly seen than in the open-air. Thomas Huxley was an outspoken, well-known agnostic. As an older man, staying in a country house, he saw several guests leaving to go to church one Sunday morning. He did not go, but he did approach a man with a simple, radiant faith saying, 'Suppose you don't go to church today. Suppose you stay and tell me why you are a Christian and what your faith means to you.' 'But', the man replied, 'you could demolish my arguments in a minute. I am not clever enough to argue with you.' Huxley gently replied, 'I don't want to argue with you; I just want you to tell me what your Christ means to you.' The man stayed and did as Huxley had requested. When he finished, there were tears in the agnostic's eyes, though, as far as I know, he never turned to the Lord.

We have a unique Saviour, and as personal workers we are not to be 'Jesuses' to people but ambassadors and witnesses pointing to Him. We are sinners. He is the Saviour. And, as such, He is able to meet the deepest needs of any individual.

As we engage people in conversation:

- present His sinlessness to transgressors;

- present His purity to the immoral;

- present His truthfulness to the dishonest;

- present His abundant life to the empty;

- present His sincerity to the deceivers;

- present His humility to the proud; and

- present His death and resurrection to all.

- present Jesus, the friend of sinners, who came to seek and save the lost.

But how does a conversation start? It begins with intentionality. In your morning 'quiet time', pray that God would make opportunities for you to witness. Then go into the day looking for them. Pray for those who stop to listen at the open-air that you might be able to speak to them. Pray that God will not only cause people to be receptive to taking Christian literature from you but talking to you about it.

There are two types of people. The first are the people we meet regularly, our colleagues, neighbours, friends. Pray for them by name and pray for the right opportunity to chat with them. Ideally it will be in a one-to-one situation, but take the moment when it comes. It is good to ask questions and seek to understand them and what they are thinking, but be sure to keep to the main issue— the gospel!

On the other hand, there are many people we will never meet again. We meet them on a bus or train; they serve us in a supermarket, stand next to us at a bus queue or we meet them in the open-air. Just talk! Talk about the weather, the long wait for the bus to come, anything, but just chatter in a warm way, and seek to mention your faith or your church, or a Christian view of whatever is concerning them. Don't ram the gospel at them but, in a winsome way, ask them about themselves and speak of Jesus.

In an open-air context, be on the lookout for those who have shown an interest in what is going on. They are not always so obvious. Sometimes people observe from a distance. Approach them in a friendly manner and enquire if they have any thoughts on Christian things or what they have heard in the preaching. This can be a gentle way into a one-to-one conversation about the Lord Jesus.

I have found gospel tracts to be the key to open many a door to conversation. If no one is waiting behind me at a supermarket check-out, offering with a smile, a 'little Christian leaflet that you might enjoy' maybe the opening to further chat. I never go anywhere without a wallet full of various tracts, and seek to use them, or if need be, lose them by leaving them in a place which isn't going to be a nuisance but will be found. On the streets, politely offering a Christian leaflet to passers-by can also unlock a conversation.

The greatest act of friendship I can show anyone is to introduce them to Jesus and the greatest act of tyranny is to know the gospel and yet not pass it on. Ask yourself if your neighbour knows the gospel. They know you go to church and that you are 'religious', but do they know the gospel? The sin of the rich man in the story of the rich man and Lazarus was that he neglected his neighbour. May we never be guilty of doing the same. The gospel is not to be hidden but proclaimed, shared, chatted about and made known to those we meet regularly and those we may never see again.

Invite a friend for a coffee and cake; get to know them; invite them to a gospel service at your church, talk with them about Jesus. If you have grandchildren, treat them to a good pizza and a great night out, and ask them about their faith. Let them know of your love for them and your prayers for them.

> *Lead me to some soul today*
> *and teach me Lord just what to say.*
> *Friends of mine are lost in sin*
> *and cannot find the way.*
> *Few there are, and few who pray,*
> *so melt my heart and fill my life*
> *to win some soul today.*

A good discipline for any personal worker is to learn verses of Scripture. Having memorised helpful texts, we can then draw on them in our conversation to back up what we are saying. For example, when explaining that salvation is not based on what we can do, you could quote verses like; 'Knowing that a man is not justified by the works of the law but by faith in Jesus Christ...' (Galatians 2:16a); or, 'For by grace you have been saved through faith, and that not of yourselves; it is the gift of God, not of works, lest anyone should boast' (Ephesians 2:8-9). Of course, we have a Bible full of verses, but the point is, unless we know them we cannot use them in our dialogue with people. Someone once said, 'The Holy Spirit will lead and prompt you with verses of Scripture to use in conversation, but unless you know them, that would have to be a miracle!'

7. The Programme

Whilst we 'fly the flag' for open-air preaching as a valid way of engaging the masses with the gospel in the 21st Century, it is not the only way of connecting with people. We must not play down the primacy of preaching but neither must we dismiss other legitimate methods at our disposal.

Typically, an open-air would consist of three main components:

- **Preaching**—short bursts of engaging preaching, each around 10–15 minutes in duration.

- **Literature distribution**—offering tracts ('tracting') to those passing by, ideally 'down-stream' of the open-air.

- **One-to-one conversations**—talking to people who have shown an interest, applying the gospel to them as individuals in the context of a private conversation.

Each of these components should complement one another rather than hinder or distract. How could legitimate gospel methods hinder or disturb an open-air? Picture the scene, a passer-by stops to listen to the preach—great! But then, an excited Christian sees they have stopped to listen and thrusts a leaflet under their nose.

Are you Good Enough to go to Heaven?

They've now been distracted from listening to the preacher and, more often than not, end up walking away! Or, another scenario. Picture a Christian engaging a non-Christian in conversation right in front of the display board as the preacher is trying to preach around them! How about another scenario? All the helpers are handing out tracts and there is no-one to support and encourage the preacher—nor create the environment conducive to encouraging people to stop and listen! All of these have happened—and can easily happen! So, let us make sure these three integral parts of an open-air work do complement each other rather than undermine the programme.

Depending on those who are assisting in the open-air, other things may be considered to enhance the opportunity:

Singing

A solo or a group signing a clear gospel hymn (rather than a 'worship song' relevant only to Christians) can add something to a witness. This is particularly true at Christmas time with the singing of carols. It is worth noting that well-meaning Christians aren't necessarily the best judge of 'good' singing. I've been in some situations where I have visibly grimaced as high notes have been missed or old-favourites have been massacred! Please, if we are to use singing in our witness, make sure it is good!

Testimonies

This is a great way of including other Christians in the open-air. They may not be a preacher, but they can share their testimony publicly. Although we believe it is exclusively the man's role to preach, a testimony can happily incorporate a lady in this capacity and use her conversion story to the benefit of the open-air. However, rather than someone just standing up and reminiscing, the best practice is to have an experienced open-air preacher lead the testimony. That means they can 'interview' the person and control where the testimony goes, ensuring it always comes back to the gospel. It is also beneficial for the interviewer to repeat the answers should the one giving their testimony be a little quieter of voice. The obvious benefit of controlling the interview like this is to ensure it is short, sharp and to the point!

Questionnaires

I am also dubious about surveys on the streets and often avoid people with a clipboard like the plague! Yet, I do know many have had meaningful conversations as a result of a carefully constructed questionnaire. If questionnaires are to be used, the important thing to remember in this regard is transparency. Be up front about who you are—we are not into subtlety or deception. Make sure those you are trying to engage know you are a Christian and, in an age where GDPR is so prevalent, ensure they know *why* you are gathering information. For these reasons, beware of asking personal questions but ask leading questions concerning their thoughts about God, Jesus Christ or the Bible; questions that can be a 'springboard' to easily explain the gospel, without the person feeling duped or 'hard-done-by'.

Question of the day

This can be particularly useful on a display board where preaching is not possible or appropriate. Displaying a question of the day is a 'hook' to try and engage people in conversation— getting straight to the point. Questions like, 'Do good people go to Heaven?' or 'Did Jesus really come back to life?' Again, you must be upfront about who you are as Christians.

Some have developed this concept further by making it more interactive. For example, getting the passer-by to 'do something' rather than just 'say something'. I've seen this done to great effect with coloured ping-pong balls. The person is asked to place a coloured ball in one of three glass vases— 'YES', 'NO' or 'DON'T KNOW'. Once they have physically engaged in the exercise it is sometimes easier to develop a conversation with them. The added visual impact of the results can also be helpful as a talking-point.

Other ways of engagement

I've known of open-air opportunities put on by churches and organisations at carnivals or fairgrounds where they use sticky-notes. The title on a board reads, 'If you could ask God one question, what would it be?' The individual is then invited to write their response on a yellow 'post-it note' to put on the board. This can also be revealing as to where the person 'is at' and be helpful catalyst to answering their question.

In tourist areas, especially those frequented by international travellers, visitors are asked to place a pin in a world map to indicate where they are from. This can be quite interesting to see, but the challenge is to ensure transparency and a lead in to the gospel. This needs to be thought through carefully. However, I have seen this done to good effect.

Question and answer sessions

These can be public, taking questions from passers-by to put to a Christian to answer or, sometimes, putting specific questions to them on behalf of the public. Questions like, 'Has science disproved God?' or 'Isn't the Bible made-up?' can stimulate engagement and lead to applying the gospel in the answers given.

In such situations, you have to be prepared for any question and so it would only be wise to have an experienced Christian to field the questions.

Displaying 'Frequently Asked Questions' on the board is often helpful, inviting passers-by to pick one. This can also be a way of engaging passers-by individually rather than publicly.

Free literature tables

Evangelist Paul Linnell, a strong advocate of a free literature table, writes:

Including a table with free gospel literature adds much to open-air witness, increasing the 'presence' and impact of the witness. It is flexible, of course, and can be used in other settings, especially where open-air preaching is not possible.

The primary advantage is that it creates an additional contact point. It is a gentler attraction, perfectly complementing the more direct action of the preaching. Curious passers-by will stop to see what is on offer, and can be engaged through an opening question: 'Is there anything here that interests you?' Others will stop to ask about spiritual matters or to speak with a Christian. In an open-air meeting, having listened to the preaching, I've found people will often gravitate towards the table.

Additionally, it allows you to offer a greater range of evangelistic literature (in different languages too) and also promotes the active involvement of team members who are non-preachers. The ladies on the team are often best at organising the table and engaging with enquirers through it.

A lightweight folding camping table is ideal. Avoid wooden pasting tables as they are too long, not weatherproof, tend to sag and look disreputable very quickly. Make sure the table is accessible to all, including children and wheelchair/mobility-scooter users.

Choose the range of literature carefully. Make sure your team knows what is available and are familiar with the contents of the table. Keep the emphasis on the gospel. Related issues on the 'big questions', 'why all the suffering?', 'creation versus evolution' etc. are essential, and there is much excellent material available.

But it is important to ensure the main message from the table is the gospel of Christ Jesus. We want sinners to be saved by knowing Christ, not just being informed on Christian ethics. The same applies to

> **It is important to ensure the main message from the table is the gospel of Christ Jesus**

religions; there are very good specific booklets aimed at these, but ultimately all must know the person of the Lord Jesus. If space is limited, essential literature includes John's Gospels (English and other languages prevalent locally), gospel tracts on the person and work of Christ, and *Ultimate Questions* (by John Blanchard), something for children/young people, CDs of a gospel being read (for non-readers) and personal testimonies.

When arranging your literature, make sure the titles are visible! If you overlap literature because you have too much, people won't read them. Think—what are people seeing? Lay it out neatly, putting smaller items at the front and larger at the back. Clear plastic literature racks lend more space. Don't put everything out; keep a separate waterproof plastic tub for specific items. Make sure your team know where this is. Protect your literature from the elements; paper and the outdoors are not great together! Keep the literature in good condition—bundle multiple copies together with an elastic band (which also stops them blowing away!); keep an eye out for rain and have a transparent plastic sheet plus some spring clips handy. Put over-handled and worn leaflets in the recycling bin (perhaps for the recycling staff to read!).

A literature table lends itself to a banner. However, whilst it is appropriate to have a church name or organisation displayed, we are not proclaiming our church or organisation. Make sure contact information is clearly visible. People are suspicious of organisations promoting themselves, suspecting they are after their money. The table must communicate 'Come to Christ', not 'Come to us'! A bold gospel Scripture text is often all that is needed. The curious will ask, 'Who are you...?' which is a great lead into a gospel conversation.

There are, of course, other ways you may think of to try and engage people with the gospel—the list above is far from comprehensive. However, not all may be wise or appropriate to use. Anything that is not transparent or lures people in under false-pretences must be avoided (magic, gimmicks etc.). Drama can often draw a crowd on the street, but the message it is

> **Anything that is not transparent or lures people in under false-pretences must be avoided**

trying to convey is not always clear to spectators (especially those who stop part-way through). In my experience, people who have stopped to watch a sketch or a magic trick are often disgruntled to find out it was a Christian presentation and walk away before hearing the epilogue. We are not in the business of conning people into listening. A God-honouring transparency about who we are and what we are proclaiming is always the best policy. When people know we are Christians sharing the Christian message, surely it is more of an indication of real interest when they do stop? Can we say with the Apostle Paul, 'But we have renounced the hidden things of shame, not walking in craftiness nor handling the word of God deceitfully, but by manifestation of the truth commending ourselves to every man's conscience in the sight of God' (2 Corinthians 4:2).

It is good for the open-air leader to have in mind what methods he will employ in the programme, especially to give those taking part a chance to prepare. However, we are not process driven and we must be open to changing our plans based upon what is happening during the open-air. For example, a preacher may have been 'drilling for oil' and found very little response. If you haven't 'struck oil', let someone else drill. A preacher may have a heckler which moves him from his message to an impromptu question session. Be sensitive to the prompting of the Holy Spirit.

> **If you haven't 'struck oil', let someone else drill**

What about praying in the open-air?

It is sometimes good to have a short prayer together prior to commencing the witness on the street—'short' being the operative word as the priority is not a believer's prayer meeting but a gospel opportunity for unbelievers. Although we are not ashamed to pray in the open-air, we mustn't give the impression we are exclusive in a 'holy huddle' and therefore cannot be approached. By experience, the best prayer times are before we even step foot onto the street.

I would certainly discourage praying publicly. The open-air meeting is not a church service outside. Christians pray because, through Christ, they are in communion with God. Non-Christians are not in that relationship and so the priority is not to pray publicly, but to publicly explain how Jesus is the key to that relationship with God. I can remember hearing a loud, public prayer at an open-air. Whilst it was awkward for some, others just didn't have a clue what was going on and those who had shown an interest in the gospel simply slipped away whilst the believers' eyes were shut!

8. The Preparation

J ust because this chapter is the eighth in this publication, doesn't negate the importance of preparation. The English poet wrote in 1709, 'Fools rush in where angels fear to tread.' Whilst there is nothing particularly spiritual about that line, it is, nevertheless, a warning to us. It is foolish to have rushed in to any form of outreach without having first put in meaningful spiritual and practical preparation. Athletes train and prepare for months in advance. Pulpit preachers (we hope!) prepare for days in advance. Gospel workers should also be disciplined in their preparation. Is it not reasonable to assume, the more you put in, the more you get out of something? Is it not also reasonable to assume God's blessing will fall on those things which glorify Him from start to finish?

Personal time

Do you start each day with that quiet time before the Lord? This should not be seen as a 'box ticking' exercise—'Gotta get my quiet time in!' Nor are we slaves to religious ritual. As we read in Lamentations, 'Through the LORD's mercies we are not consumed, because His compassions fail not. They are new every morning; Great is Your faithfulness. "The LORD is my portion," says my soul, "Therefore I hope in Him!"' (Lamentations 3:22–24). If the Lord's mercies are new every morning, is it not fitting to start each day with a fresh reminder of His great mercy and faithfulness to us? Is it not appropriate in response to such grace that we affirm our love, loyalty and obedience to Him?

A private, personal time spent with the Lord is never time wasted. What a great way to start any day, let alone a day spent in consecrated service. But time is precious and all too easily filled with legitimate, but pressing, matters, which is why we must discipline ourselves in this regard.

I have a morning routine which seems to work for me: *Get up, have a 'wake-up' mug of coffee whilst looking at the news, read and pray, before a shower and breakfast takes me on into the day.* I have found, having 'woken up' I am better placed to digest what I am reading and pray through some of the main themes from the passage. But not everyone is like me and I am not like everyone else. The point is, we must find a time that works well for us and be disciplined in it. Ah, you say, 'I'm not a morning person'! Fine, be an evening person instead. Prepare for the day ahead by spending meaningful, personal time in the Scriptures.

> Prepare for the day ahead by spending meaningful, personal time in the Scriptures

Family-worship is important—reading and praying as a family, but don't neglect your own spiritual diet. Ministry and Bible studies in church are vital, but our souls need more to thrive. The godly man of Psalm 1 meditated on God's law both day and night. All too many of us rush into the day with little personal preparation. That is foolish.

Since becoming Christians, we must remember that God's enemy is now our enemy. Satan would seek to discourage, disrupt and destroy gospel work and gospel workers. John Wesley recorded in his journal, 'I preached at 8 am at an open place. Many were there who never did and never would come to the [meeting] room. Oh, what a victory would Satan gain if he could put an end to field-preaching!' (*Journal*, May 20th

1759). Whoever commits themselves to this work can be sure that they are in a spiritual battle, the intensity of which they may not have yet experienced. This spiritual warfare should impress upon us the need to personally prepare ourselves daily for battle.

'Christian service means invading a battleground, not a playground; and you and I are the weapons God uses to attack and defeat the enemy' (Warren Wiersbe, *On Being a Servant of God*). God hasn't left us naked or defenceless. As the Apostle Paul urged the Christians at Ephesus, 'Finally, my brethren, be strong in the Lord and in the power of His might. Put on the whole armour of God, that you may be able to stand against the wiles of the devil. For we do not wrestle against flesh and blood, but against principalities, against powers, against the rulers of the darkness of this age, against spiritual hosts of wickedness in the heavenly places. Therefore take up the whole armour of God, that you may be able to withstand in the evil day, and having done all, to stand' (Ephesians 6:10–13). Commenting on this, William Gurnall wrote, 'Now in these words he explains himself, and shows how he would have them do this, not presumptuously [to] come into the field without that armour which God hath appointed to be worn by all his soldiers, and yet with a bravado, to trust to the power of God to save them' (*The Christian in Complete Armour*).

Prayer time

James Montgomery's hymn, 'Prayer is the soul's sincere desire, unuttered or expressed' has a verse which begins, 'Prayer is the Christian's vital breath, the Christian's native air'. Is that not true? Not only is communion with God before the throne of grace essential for the believer, but it is most natural. We have free access through the Lord Jesus Christ to boldly approach our Father in Heaven, assured of his listening ear.

Prayer takes on added significance when we are engaged in gospel work. Out 'on the coal face' or 'on the front line' (as it has been described) we are more obviously reminded of the words of Jesus, 'For without me you can do nothing' (John 15:5b). In prayer then, we demonstrate our complete and utter dependence upon the Lord. We need Him, by His Spirit, to work in us and through us. We need Him to work in the hearts and lives of those we will meet. So, we ask, we petition, we beseech … we pray! After all, 'Unless the LORD builds the house, they labour in vain who build it' (Psalm 127:1a).

Prayer takes on added significance when we are engaged in gospel work

Prayer for our gospel endeavours should naturally form part of our personal prayer time. But the Christian does not live in isolation. We have been adopted into a family. We have brothers and sisters in Christ. We are part of a church. If we are under the God-given authority of a local church (which is right and proper for us to be) then are we encouraging our church family to pray? Praying for us as those involved in witnessing for Christ; praying for gospel opportunities; praying for those contacted in evangelism; praying that God would be glorified in the saving of precious souls? Some of our brothers and sisters may not be directly involved in that particular outreach but they can be involved corporately by seeking God's blessing in prayer.

Not only do we belong to a church family, we are part of a team of others (or should be—we are not 'lone-rangers'!). So, with those we are working alongside in evangelism, there is a place for focused prayer before venturing onto the streets. I can think of numerous examples where I have been so encouraged and 'fired up' by a time of prayer with the team that I could hardly wait to get out there (if only that was always true!). But I can think of equally as many encouragements when we have prayed together after an open-air—in praise for answered prayer, in supplication for those contacted.

Practical time

Spiritual preparation is important, but so too is practical preparation. Sometimes we can be guilty of being so ill-disciplined that we rush out of the door, late for an open-air, and we forget something! We must discipline ourselves to ensure that we have everything we need and that we are on time (poor time-keeping is not God-honouring, nor is it helpful if you have others working alongside you).

I knew someone who led open-airs regularly who loved camping holidays. I observed him once coming back from a camping trip. His house and garden were a mess! He had laid everything out, to dry out, sort out and fill out—so that he could pack it away ready for its next outing. It then occurred to me that same discipline he used in returning from holiday was what he practised after every open-air. Everything would be tidied, sorted, and replenished so that it was ready for the next open-air.

There is nothing worse than being ill-prepared. I have been at open-airs where we have run out of literature. I've been frustrated having to stand at an open-air

> There is nothing worse than being ill-prepared

when a preacher's visual aids were in the wrong order and he had to take valuable witnessing time to sort it out! The list of distractions could go on. I'm not perfect in this regard, but I always seek to learn from mistakes.

Prior to entering full-time Christian work I was a shop manager. When ordering stock (much to the dismay of head office) I had a motto, 'Better looking at it than for it!' In other words, if we had it in stock we could potentially sell it—but if it wasn't there, even the best salesperson couldn't sell it! When we go out into the open-air, have we got enough gospel literature with us? If it's not there, we can't give it out. We don't want to have to use a wheelbarrow to carry so much with us, but neither do we want to run out!

The Scout movement had a famous motto, 'Be prepared.' Whether it be in time-keeping, ensuring we have everything we need, or knowing where we need to be—is that our motto? Be prepared!

9. The Partners

Who are we going to stand with, shoulder-to-shoulder, in the gospel? We should only be co-labourers with those who are in full agreement with the fundamentals of the gospel. Whether they be from our own church or other Bible-believing, gospel-preaching churches, we should develop healthy links to strengthen the work.

Evangelist Andy Little writes...

The apostle Paul said, 'I thank my God ... for your fellowship in the gospel from the first day until now' (Philippians 1:3–5). This fellowship or partnership in the gospel is encouraging to believers and effective in reaching unbelievers. It may take various forms and will depend upon people's circumstances. It may include prayer, supporting, distributing literature, preaching, personal conversations or follow-up work. There is a place for everyone in open-air work. The person who simply stands to listen is doing a great job in encouraging the speaker and encouraging the public to stand and listen to this interesting speaker as well.

Many of us know the common caricature of open-air evangelism where one lone enthusiast holds a big Bible and shouts at people whilst they walk past without any interest. By contrast, a group of people listening to an interesting and relevant speaker presenting a message with clarity and sincerity, can encourage people to stop and listen. In the book of Acts we see that the Apostle Paul almost always operated with a known team.

The purpose of partnership for believers

- **A deeper sense of unity with God's people:** secondary issues remain such when we work together for the salvation of sinners.

- **Fuel for prayer:** church prayer meetings light up when people pray for individuals who have heard the gospel.

- **Opportunities to exercise gifts:** many come away from an open-air meeting thrilled that they were able to speak to someone about their Saviour. This may be the first time for some and may be something that they never thought they would be able to do.

- **Development in our walk with the Lord:** we discover the truth of the great commission: that when we go, He is with us.

- **Increasing confidence in the gospel:** we discover that God is still reaching lost people in our culture today.

- **An increased gospel presence:** many churches cannot afford to employ an evangelist or organise an open-air meeting, but they can partner with someone else who is willing to lead one.

The purpose of partnership for the public

- **The credibility of the speaker:** he does not just look like a lone person without any associates.

- **Encouragement to listen:** not many want to be the first to stand and listen. It is much easier to stand among others.

- **Representation:** when young and old, male and female, stand together in the gospel, it is a great representation of gospel truth, that we are one in Christ and that the gospel is for people from all different backgrounds.

- **Efficiency:** while one preaches, another is able to speak to people personally, another is able to show people the available literature and another is able to pray with someone.

- **Prayer:** believers are on hand and are able to pray for the immediate situation (i.e. for those listening or when a person asks questions of the speaker).

Developing this partnership

- **Pray:** ask the Lord to provide workers to work together in the gospel (Luke 10:2).

- **Write:** to churches and individuals that you know in the area where the witness will take place. We do this for several reasons:

  * *Courtesy*—*to them as we plan to work in their area.*

  * *Prayer*—*we need their prayers and concern.*

  * *Encouragement*—*they may be thrilled that the Lord has sent help.*

  * *Involvement*—*they may want to join the witness. They may have useful church literature and invites that can be used with interested people.*

- **Seminars:** these are a good format to present the work, raise interest, present needs and answer any questions or concerns that people may have.

- **Organise:** with others explore the situation and then plan to hold an open-air meeting.

- **Report:** the book of Acts shows us that the apostles reported back on the work of the gospel. People will be encouraged to hear about what happened. This will then result in prayer and further interest.

- **Advance:** consider with interested partners how further opportunities may be taken. These may involve other locations, new literature and special times such as Christmas and Easter. An open-air witness in the day could be linked to an evangelistic meeting in a local church in the evening. It may also be possible to join a mission event such as those organised by United Beach Missions, Christian Answer, The Open-Air Mission or Open-Air Campaigners etc.

- **Training:** we all need to regularly think through our best practices. Subjects may include, preaching, handing out literature, personal conversations, dealing with questions, praying with people, visual aids etc.

- **Pray:** have special prayer meetings for all those who attend, those who are interested and for those who faithfully pray for the work. There are some believers who are not able to attend but who are faithful prayer warriors.

How you can be a discouragement:	How you can be an encouragement:
• Be critical	• Be helpful
• Turn up late	• Be on time
• Never pray for them	• Be prayerful
• Chat during the preaching	• Be focused
• Don't bother going	• Be faithful

10. The Practical Stuff

Have you ever noticed the solicitors' adverts for a no-win, no-fee compensation claim? 'Have you been involved in an accident that wasn't your fault? Then you could be entitled to compensation!' This blame-claim culture of ours has forced an increased awareness of health and safety and insurance cover. After all, no one wants to be sued—'Where there's a blame, there's a claim'! We may roll our eyes at the thought of the 'nanny-state' imposing such things as a risk assessment upon us, but, actually, they are quite useful.

Local authorities (or their contracted agencies) are often keen to know that what is happening on the streets will not 'come back to bite them'. In other words, they want to know that street entertainers, buskers, vendors and the like, are not going to cause an injury, potentially bringing liability and negative publicity upon the council. Any apparatus we use on the streets should have been assessed and be covered by the relevant insurances etc.

Risk assessments

A risk assessment is exactly that. Risks relating to a particular object or event have been assessed. Having highlighted probable and even improbable hazards, mitigating measures have been put in place. For example, a free literature table— could someone inadvertently trip over the table leg? That is a risk. Now, knowing that hazard, what can we do to avoid it? Affixing black and yellow hazard tape to the table legs increases its visibility and means it is now less likely to be a risk. What about the table or display board blowing away and hitting someone in strong winds? A reasonable measure to counter that risk is to ensure that it is tied to something or weighted down.

Identify the potential risk and list the action taken to guard against it. That, in a nutshell, is a risk assessment. Should any local authority worker approach you, having a copy of this document will help put their legitimate concerns at ease.

Health and safety

We can put in place all the policies and procedures in the world, but if we have them we should be committed to them. In other words, if we have said we will do something in a document, then do it we must! We, of all people, should display honesty and integrity. Having established a risk assessment, ensure all the team are briefed in it.

But policies and procedures are no substitute for common-sense! Ensure that all those taking part in the open-air are wise in what they are doing. Be aware of health and safety—*are we operating safely? Could any valid concerns be raised about our operations?* If so, please deal with those issues. What a shame we could bring on the gospel if we are reckless or neglectful in the open-air. We pray that accidents don't happen, but if they do, let us be seen to have acted wisely and taken all reasonable precautions. Maintaining a good testimony is crucial.

Both national government and devolved administrations have help online in compiling a relevant risk assessment. Risk assessment templates can also be downloaded from various sources.

Insurance

The benefit of being affiliated to an organisation is that they (should) provide all necessary cover for their workers and associates. If an incident occurs and someone wants to make a claim against you (for example, a personal injury as a result of a display board falling on someone) then their public liability insurance policy will respond. Such organisations also have employer's liability—they are required to by law if they have employees. This covers claims against them should an employee or volunteer be injured.

If you are not part of an organisation then you need to ensure that you have cover—just in case. Again, local authorities take a dim view of potential damages which may implicate them. So, having appropriate cover in place will ensure their fears are allayed. This does highlight the benefit of being part of an established group rather than a 'lone ranger'.

Public liability insurance can be obtained for a regular work on the streets or a one-off event. Most policy applications will require a thorough risk assessment, otherwise insurance companies will not have the confidence to entrust you with cover. It is worth noting that some local authorities require a minimum indemnity limit (particularly for one-off events), for example, of £5,000,000.

If you are going out under the banner of your church, then it is worth checking that the church insurance policy covers organised events beyond the church premises (i.e. on the streets). If so, then check what that policy requires of you to ensure the cover will respond in the event of a claim. You should check that the cover provided is adequate or seek advice to arrange appropriate cover with a recognised insurer. This is a specialist area of knowledge and you should always consult an insurance professional for advice.

There are other practical implications to open-air work which need to be considered. Warnings and exhortations—things to beware of and things to do to maximise the opportunity in the open-air:

Team members

If preaching is an important component in an open-air, surely we should try to create an environment conducive for people to listen. Picture the scene: the preacher is preaching his heart out, but his Christian supporters are idly chatting amongst themselves:

- *What encouragement is that for people to stop and listen to his message?*

- *How discouraging to the preacher that even the Christians are not interested in what he is saying!*

So, there are positive things the team can do during the preaching:

- **Listen!** If you are not listening, how can you expect others to?

- **Look interested!** If you are interested, that will encourage the preacher and help towards attracting the interest of others to his message.

- **Look out!** During the preaching, keep a look out for those who may have stopped (but be discreet!). You will be able to gently sidle up to them afterwards (or after they walk away) to try and get into conversation.

But there are things which the team shouldn't do during the preaching:

- **Don't talk!** Whether it is talking to fellow Christians or interested parties, it can distract people from listening. It can also distract and discourage the preacher. If you are to get into conversation, do so away from the preaching area so as not to hinder others listening.

- **Don't tract!** Don't offer tracts to those who are listening (as mentioned in chapter 7), wait until the preacher has finished or the listener moves away.

Remember, if they are listening, let them listen! While people are listening to the preaching, they are learning from the Word of God. Let us seek to ensure everything we do in the open-air creates an atmosphere whereby people are encouraged to listen.

There is also something very practical, but extremely helpful to consider about the team—where will they stand during the preaching? We don't want a 'Great Wall of China' in front of the preacher, meaning that folk are almost like Zacchaeus, unable to see past them! (See figure 1.) Neither do we want the team flanking the preacher as in a political rally, all looking out towards anyone who has the courage to stop and listen—how intimidating! (See figure 2.) If anything, that practice does more to exclude than include people.

By experience, we have learned to stand not too far away from the preacher (but not too close either!). It is best to ensure that Christians are not in a formal line, but randomly situated in front of the preacher. (See figure 3.) This creates a less intimidating and a more welcoming scenario, which is more conducive to people stopping to listen. Also, this makes it easier to follow up the listeners once the preacher has finished.

Figure 1 How not to stand in the open-air

Figure 2 How not to stand in the open-air

Figure 3 How best to stand in the open-air

Entrapment

'The fear of man brings a snare, but whoever trusts in the LORD shall be safe' (Proverbs 29:25). Fearing people's reaction can be a real hindrance to opening our mouths to share the gospel. More so when those people may be laying a trap of their own in which to catch us out. Even the Lord Jesus had people posing questions to Him, trying to get Him to say something by which they could accuse Him.

Entrapment is being lured into saying something that can then be turned into an accusation against us.

The 'hot potatoes' are gender issues and sexual orientation. Wisdom is crucial. Whilst we do not want to unnecessarily rile people and cause a stir we must be faithful to God's Word. A balanced approach, as previously stated, is vitally important.

It is good practice for an open-air preacher to record his preaching. This can be done discreetly on a phone or an mp3 voice recorder, discreetly located in your pocket. Personally, I avoid body-cams and other such cameras. In my experience, people generally avoid being on camera and so that can be detrimental to drawing people in to listen. It can also be viewed as antagonistic, 'gunning for a fight'. Plus, if we are operating what could be construed as 'CCTV' then signage should declare that—another potential hindrance to our outreach. Rather, something discreet recording your speech is a good back up. There have been instances when a complaint has been made to the police about what a preacher has said. Thankfully, the preacher was able to produce the recording to verify that they had not said or done anything illegal.

Some helpful advice I learnt years ago was to apply the 'R H Factor'. When someone asks a potentially loaded question, ask yourself – 'Is this a "Red Herring"?' as in, are they just trying to throw me off topic? Or, 'Is this a Real Hindrance to them?' Weighing up the motives behind the question will help us respond accordingly. Red herrings are just a distraction and not worth pursuing, but real hindrances, on the other hand, are worth pursuing in order to apply the gospel.

But in all these things, the best advice is to keep the main thing the main thing!

Code of conduct

Not only should all participants at an open-air be briefed in matters relating to health and safety, thought should also be given to other practical and spiritual scenarios. Sometimes, it is good to compile a short, but clear, code of conduct to ensure everyone is 'singing from the same hymn sheet'. Things to consider are:

- How best to contact people on the street.

- Ensuring we 'major on the majors' and not get side-tracked on secondary issues.

- How best to counsel someone.

- Who to refer people to (for practical or pastoral support).

- What is the best literature to offer.

- Which church(es) to recommend.

- What to do if someone indicates they would like to trust the Lord Jesus as their Saviour.

The list can go on and should be based upon the particular context you are in. It doesn't have to be a written document, but verbal training. The point is, everyone should be aware of such things so that we all work together without anyone or anything undermining that work.

Street evangelism and the law

Sam Webster, Solicitor Advocate of the Christian Institute, writes:

> There is no right to say whatever we like at the time and place of our choosing. But the European Court of Human Rights has ruled that, subject to matters such as the proper maintenance of public order, free speech includes information or ideas 'that offend, shock or disturb'. And in 1999 Lord Justice Sedley famously ruled that free speech includes:

'not only the inoffensive but the irritating, the contentious, the eccentric, the heretical, the unwelcome and the provocative provided it does not tend to provoke violence. Freedom only to speak inoffensively is not worth having.'[1]

The Public Order Act 1986 protects the public from harassment, alarm and distress, but it does not confer a right merely not to be offended. Rather, it tackles speech which is threatening, abusive or insulting. Preaching Christ should be none of those things. That said, there is a risk that people may feel (or claim to feel) insulted by hearing about their need for a saviour. However, insults are caught only if they cause and are intended to cause harassment alarm or distress. This means that allegations are more likely to arise where speech is directed to a specific person. What is more, it is a defence if a person's conduct was reasonable. The gospel challenges and may cause offence, but responsible evangelism cannot fairly be characterised as offensive. The fruit of the Spirit includes gentleness and in Philippians 4:5 we are reminded to let our gentleness (or reasonableness) be known to all.

Our excellent free speech laws are also reflected in anti-litter laws. On public land, free Christian literature can generally be distributed without the need for permission from the local authority. The Environmental Protection Act 1990 exempts religious literature from the limitations on the distribution of free material which may be imposed under that Act.

---

1 Redmond-Bate v Director of Public Prosecutions [1999] EWHC Admin 733
   (23 July 1999) at para 20.

But with rights go responsibilities. So here are a few tips to avoid unnecessary opposition:

- Ground all preaching in Scripture.

- Commend the exclusive claims of Jesus rather than preaching against other faiths.

- Be wise. Some topics, such as sexual ethics, should be tackled with care, and in the appropriate context. Remember Christ's words to the woman caught in adultery.

- Be Christ-like in response to challenges. Friendly cooperation and good humour can defuse a difficult situation and be a good witness. A street preacher's reasonableness may give a police officer the confidence to do the right thing.

- Avoid using displays in areas of highly concentrated pedestrian flow to avoid obstruction and be sensitive to the needs of other users.

- Check for local by-laws, such as Public Spaces Protection Orders, which might impose restrictions on what can be done in the area. But it is rare for them to interfere with free speech. If in doubt, contact The Christian Institute for advice.

- Keep away from privately owned property.

- Know your rights and don't hesitate to challenge any misuse of the law.

- Keep an audio or video recording of your preaching in the open-air, in case a complaint is made.

Further guidance on free speech and street evangelism can be obtained from The Christian Institute at: https://www.christian.org.uk or by emailing LDF@christian.org.uk.

Questions

Posing questions to those we engage with the gospel is good practice—why? Because when you ask a question, it prompts a thought-process and response—doesn't it? But what about questions put to us? Even experienced evangelists can have questions fired at them that they have never experienced before. Many questions can be answered generally, keeping to the main themes of the gospel. But, if you do not know the answer to specific question, say so! People can generally recognise when someone is 'blagging'. Honesty is always the best policy. But did you realise, not knowing an answer can be helpful?

Not only does honesty display integrity on your part, it can provide further contact with that person. 'I'm sorry, I'm not sure how best to answer that question right now. Would you let me research that and give you a more thought-through response?' If they are a serious enquirer, they will accept this. Arrange to swap contact details (either of the organisation, church, or personal email/mobile number—but beware of giving away your home address or phone number). Sometimes arranging to meet the next time you are in the open-air is the best policy.

Having answered the question, you are better placed to take that question in the future! But it is a good exercise to think through questions you may be asked and how you would answer them. Such questions make Bible study more meaningful to us. One of the exciting elements of open-air work is that you do not know what is going to be asked next!

Amplification

A question I am often asked is, 'Do you use amplification when you preach in the open-air.' The simple answer is, 'No!' The rationale behind this is that there is always a tendency for the volume to be cranked up. There is also the risk of sound becoming distorted and therefore unintelligible. Amplification can keep people at a distance, when we would rather have them draw in to listen. Microphones can also give the impression of preaching 'at' someone rather than 'to' someone. The natural voice of the preacher, lifted but not strained, is sufficient to publicly declare the gospel without coming across as aggressive or antagonistic.

Of course, some circumstances mean that amplification is useful, for example, in a particularly noisy event. Sometimes, because of a limitation or weakness on the preacher's voice, a 'voice enhancer' can be used—raising the preacher's voice to that of a normal, lifted volume. In all these things, we need to ensure the volume is appropriate and that every word spoken is clear for those listening.

Literature

There is no shortage of good Christian literature available for use in an open-air context. This can be printed matter, CDs, DVDs or links to material available digitally. We can divide the categories of literature as follows:

- **Tracts/leaflets:** Something that can be given away en masse and can act as a key to unlock a gospel conversation.

- **Scriptures:** Something of God's Word to be passed on.

- **Evangelistic:** Something that explains the way of salvation.

- **Apologetic:** Something that deals with specific controversies.

- **Specific:** Something that deals with certain and particular issues.

Tracts/leaflets

The best tracts are not too 'wordy', but a simple and thought-provoking presentation of the gospel. It should have a good 'hook' on the cover and contain follow-up details at the end (as in, where should the person go to find out more?). If we are to use these, 'printed missionaries' (as a friend of mine calls them), then know what is in them! Be familiar with it, because you may end up in conversation with someone because of it! Even just the offering of a Christian leaflet can be a catalyst to a conversation about the Lord. In areas where other languages are spoken widely, you may wish to consider having some foreign literature available.

Scriptures

We are 'people of the book'. I'd rather people don't take 'my word' but 'God's Word' and so, as a matter of practice, we should always try and place a portion of Scripture into their hands. In an open-air context, with that first contact, it is not always appropriate (nor a wise use of resources) to offer a whole Bible.

Some like to offer a Luke's Gospel—written to show the certainty of what had been reported about Jesus Christ. Others like to give away Mark's Gospel, which records the first message of Jesus, 'The time is fulfilled, and the kingdom of God is at hand. Repent, and believe the gospel' (Mark 1:15). John's eyewitness account was written 'that you may believe that Jesus is the Christ, the Son of God, and that believing you may have life in His name' (John 20:31). The Open-Air Mission like to offer the latter and, every year, thousands of copies are passed on to those who want to know more.

But sometimes it is more appropriate to offer something more substantial, perhaps a New Testament and Psalms or even a whole Bible. If you haven't got anything available, then offer to send a copy—this has the advantage of further contact with the person.

Evangelistic

Someone has listened to the preaching or been spoken to in conversation, but it is not always easy to replay in your mind what has been said. This is why good evangelistic literature is important. Booklets, CDs or DVDs which convey the fundamentals of the gospel can reinforce and remind the person about what they have heard. Have a good supply of these to offer to interested parties.

Apologetics

If people have a particular interest, or it would be helpful to them in finding out the biblical stance on certain themes, then it is worth having appropriate literature. Short, but helpful, booklets on creation, as opposed to evolution, or the evidence for the empty tomb are easily sourced and should be readily available. Such items of literature are not for general distribution, rather kept for those who are open to reading more about the Christian view on such topics.

Specific

Literature that deals with certain and particular topics is also useful to have available. The question, 'If there's a God, then why is there all the suffering in the world?' is a question that often arises. Having something available that deals directly with that specific question will help the enquirer understand how we view such things from a biblical perspective. Other literature on issues such as cults, depression, gender, loneliness, occult, religions, sexuality, etc. may also be considered to speak directly into that person's situation. However, a note of caution: be wise to whom you give such literature. As mentioned above under 'Entrapment', ask yourself whether the issue raised is a real hindrance to the enquirer. If it is, then it is worth offering something they can consider in detail.

Follow-up

Over the years, I have seen many tracts and evangelistic leaflets produced by individuals, churches and Christian groups. Some of them have been very well produced in style and in substance. Sometimes, I have imagined I was a non-Christian reading through such literature. Suppose my 'appetite had been whetted', suppose I had been really stirred to find out more—what then? Some good literature I have seen has left people 'high and dry'. Make sure any gospel literature you offer has a point of contact on it, someone or somewhere enquirers can ask questions, find out more or request further literature or help. Follow-up is vital. It is always encouraging to hear back from those we have contacted on the street—either showing a deeper interest or to tell us that they have trusted the Lord as their Saviour! An appropriate following up on the former means engaging further with them. With the latter, seeking to provide them with a Bible, nurture their spiritual growth and feed them into a good local church should always be a priority.

The use of apologetics

Apologetics are reasoned arguments to justify our belief. We actually use apologetics more than we may realise in our preaching or gospel conversations. For example, when speaking of the resurrection of the Lord Jesus, we will often give the biblical evidence of eyewitnesses, who testify to having seen the risen Jesus. When we speak of the accuracy of the Bible by how Jesus fulfilled the prophecies of the Old Testament, we are using apologetics. Even when we share our testimony, we are using a reasoned argument to justify our belief in Christ.

Apologetics have an important place in presenting the gospel to an unbelieving world. They can also serve to reinforce and strengthen the faith of believers. It is always profitable to have a basic grasp of reasoned arguments for such topics as creation versus evolution, the deity of Christ, the authenticity of the Scriptures etc. These can be a blessing to our own soul, but can be used in our evangelism to help unbelievers see the validity of the Christian message.

Yet, apologetics must not take 'centre-stage'. Our helpful and pointed arguments can be a 'hook', or used to substantiate the biblical truth we share, but they must not be the sum total of our message. We may manage to sway the non-Christian with facts and figures into considering an intelligent designer or 'young earth' position, but, if we have not presented Christ, there is something fundamentally wrong! Apologetics should always lead to Christ. As a result of the reasoned argument we have presented, we use that solid foundation to share and apply the gospel.

Hecklers

Mike Mellor has dealt with the preacher's response to the heckler in chapter 4. However, what about others who are involved in the open-air? What should their response be? Firstly, do not see hecklers as a nuisance. Rather, see them as a potential blessing. Do you remember back in your school days (or perhaps it was just in my 'rough' school!) when two pupils got into an altercation? The 'hue and cry' would go out, 'Fight! Fight! Fight!' Though naturally people would be against a violent outburst, curiosity brought many in to watch! A good heckler can have the same effect—though, God-willing, without the physical nature!

A raised voice in objection to the preacher, or a question thrown out to him by a heckler, can actually be helpful. Not only has it shown that the preacher has got a reaction to his message, it can also draw others in to see how the preacher responds to such intervention. The challenge for the preacher is how he deals with it and turns it back to the gospel. But the challenge for those Christians involved in the open-air is to leave the preacher to deal with it. Naturally, we may want to respond to the heckler ourselves or even quieten them down, but that can be counter-productive. Engaging them during the preaching is a distraction and will not be helpful (nor encouraging) to the preacher.

What can you do? Pray! Pray for the preacher as he responds. Pray for the heckler to be reasonable and receptive to the response. Pray that others would be drawn to listen as a result. Pray that Christ would be honoured!

As hard as it may be, leave the preacher to deal with hecklers. He will call for help if he needs it. By all means engage a heckler once they have walked away from the area of witness. But, to create an atmosphere whereby more could potentially hear the gospel, watch and pray!

11. The Perseverance

To start out is one thing, to continue is another. There have been some gifted Christians who have embarked on witnessing in the open-air but, for a variety of reasons, have now ceased engaging in this form of outreach. Sometimes, in the providence of God, fresh doors of opportunities open to them. Others have practical reasons which forbid them. Some, however, have ground to a halt because of discouragements in the work.

David was God's anointed king over Israel, but his reign would be plagued by difficulties, even discouragements from within his own family. When his son Absalom sought to set himself up as a rival king, David fled. Psalm 3 depicts for us David's troubles but clearly shows from whence his help came. Even though so many had risen up against him, he knew God to be a shield to protect and vindicate him. Consequently, David was at peace enough to sleep. A new day would bring fresh trials, but knowing divine help, David could persevere. 'I lay down and slept; I awoke, for the LORD sustained me' (Psalm 3:5).

If we are going to continue at the 'coal face' or on the 'front line' of evangelism, then our strength and endurance can only come from the great Sustainer Himself. Persevering is not too difficult when, by God's grace, we see fruit for our labours. But what of the harder times? Who will get up in the morning to face yet more discouragements? Only the sovereign Lord will keep us going. Can we say with the psalmist, 'Our soul waits for the LORD; He is our help and our shield' (Psalm 33:20)?

Edwin Baker, the co-author of the original *Handbook on Open-Air Evangelism* shares his experience:

I was twenty-one years of age and had been converted through the testimony of a man who had faithfully given witness to Christ. Up to this point, having had no Christian influence, I gave myself to the pleasures of life. These increasingly brought disappointment to me in their failure in bringing any satisfaction. Through the witness of this dear man of God I learnt that I was a sinner and that Christ came to pay the price for my sin on the cross. He gave me gospel literature to read and, three weeks later, I made it known that I wanted to place my trust and faith in the Lord Jesus—an experience which was to revolutionise my life.

Two years later, I was married to Sandy, but only two months later she had a brain haemorrhage from which she almost died. Thankfully, the Lord spared her, though for several years she suffered the after-effects. At this time, I was working in a department store in the centre of Nottingham, and had just been promoted to a managerial position, when the clear call to proclaim Christ in the public arena was given.

In Nottingham's Market Square, just two minutes from where I worked, there were always crowds of people, taking the opportunity to listen to the various speakers who endeavoured to make their appeal to respond to their ideologies. These speakers were committed to their beliefs and spoke with passion. I remember

> These speakers were committed to their beliefs and spoke with passion

there was an elderly gentleman who belonged to the Free-Thinking Society, a convinced atheist. There was also a Communist, as well as a number of other characters. Adding to the colour of all that was going on there were several 'hecklers', who seemed to go out of their way to make fun of what was being said.

Every lunch time I would listen to these speakers and there came a growing awareness and concern since there was no Christian speaker on the scene. Here were crowds of people who gave their ears to all that was being said, yet sadly, no Christian was willing to stand up and proclaim the truth of the gospel. If ever there was an opportunity waiting to be taken, surely this must be the place! Here was a vast number who, for the most part, had no idea of their need of the

These were people going to a lost eternity— clearly an opportunity for the good news to be proclaimed!

Lord Jesus Christ. These were people going to a lost eternity—clearly an opportunity for the good news to be proclaimed! I made this a matter of prayer and made known to the Lord that I was prepared to give support to such a person who would be prepared to give himself to the task.

As time went on, no Christian appeared to take up the opportunity, and I began to get the uncomfortable feeling that the Lord was asking me to take on the challenge. Over a long period of time I excused myself from such a task. I had had no experience in public speaking, I had little knowledge of the Bible and I was relatively young in the faith (having only been a Christian for three years).

I had seen the 'hecklers' at work and wondered how I could possibly survive, and finally, there was the question of what my employers would think and how this would affect my career?

However, one big lesson I had learnt in the few years that I had been a believer was, that if you wanted to make progress in your Christian life, you must be prepared to let God have His way in your life. I had proved this on several occasions where the Lord had put His finger on certain things in my life, and it was only as I was willing to let the Lord lead that I seemed to make progress. When there were times, for one reason or another, that I was unwilling to let the Lord lead and use me, my Christian life seemed to be affected. I had now come to the point where, in spite of all the objections I had placed before the Lord, I was going to have to let Him have His way. The more I considered what Jesus had been prepared to do for me in going all the way to the cross, experiencing the humiliation, and to bear my punishment for sin— what excuse could I possibly offer in failing to respond to His call to such a work? Added to this was the way the Lord had graciously spared my wife, for which I was so grateful. So, finally, after a long struggle, I yielded up my will to the clear and unmistakable 'call' I had received.

It was one lunch time, in early May 1962, when I knew the time had now come when I must make the gospel message known in this public arena. There were three other speakers in the Market Square that day, all of whom had a crowd of people listening. The 'hecklers' were, as usual, busily engaged, seeking to make their funny comments to win the applause of onlookers.

In order to be identified as a speaker, you had to climb up onto a raised area, some two feet above the paved area. To do this for the first time seemed so hard, but eventually, after calling upon the Lord to give me strength and courage to make the step, I stood up and began to preach.

As soon as the 'hecklers' noticed there was a new man on the scene, they moved over to hear what I had to say, followed by many who had been listening to the other speakers. Before very long I must have had over two hundred people listening—not because I was an eloquent speaker, but because I was a newcomer! How would I fare with the 'hecklers', as well as many others who chipped in with their comments and questions?

A good number of the questions, I had to admit, I did not have the answer to. I simply made the best use of the answers I did have. I also used my own personal testimony of what the Lord had done for me and sought to make much of the cross. My session lasted for a good three-quarters of an hour, when I had to apologise for drawing to a close because I had to get back to work! But, I promised I would be back the next day. I had enjoyed a good listening. The Lord had been my helper and I gave thanks to Him for His enabling.

> I used my own personal testimony of what the Lord had done for me and sought to make much of the cross

The next day I was back and, in fact, every lunch time thereafter. In due time, other Christians came to help in the witness. Sometimes, one of the team would give their testimony or be prepared to be asked questions that would bring out how they had come to faith. There were times when we took on the 'hecklers', as this encouraged others to put their questions to us.

For all involved, it was a great spiritual exercise, not only from the point of view of learning how to engage the minds of those who were listening but also to communicate the gospel. The personal benefit it gave was also clear. When returning to work, we knew we had to live up to an expected standard, on account of our public profession of the Christian faith. The daily witness was to continue on in the Old Market Square for the next ten years until, in the early seventies, we moved the witness to the new pedestrianised precinct that was opened up. It was here that we found ourselves in a different situation, not having a ready-made audience. We had to learn to gain the ears of the passer-by, and so developed the use of a display board, in order to use visual aids, which proved to be a great help in causing people to stop and listen.

The daily open-airs each lunch time continued to be worthwhile opportunities for the gospel. There were times when, I have to confess, the last thing I wanted to do was go out and give myself to an open-air. There were occasions when I'd had a difficult morning, with the stresses and strains of the business I was involved with, and, as a result, one just did not feel up to the challenge.

It was at such times as these I learnt to force myself to go, regardless of how I felt. On returning to work I knew I had made the right decision and, I guess, there were times when my colleagues had the same experience. There is no doubt that these lunch time meetings kept us in touch with how ordinary folk thought. Sad to say, unbelief seemed to dominate the hearts of so many people we contacted daily. However, there were those who had an enquiring mind, which was evident by the fact that we had so many people listening. This spurred us on, and though we were plagued by our regular group of 'hecklers', there were others who came up with genuine questions that we endeavoured to answer.

Issues such as, 'Why does God allow suffering?', 'What about all the other religions?', 'Is there life after death?', 'Can the Bible be trusted?', 'What proof do we have that God really exists?' or, 'What about evolution?' All of these questions were thrown at us, as well as many more, but we gave thanks to the Lord for providing such an opportunity for the gospel. As we sought to answer each question, we made it our practice to underline the real problem—the problem of sin. From there we went on to show that the purpose of Christ's coming was to deal with the problem by His death on the cross, and that forgiveness is given to those who believe and put their trust in Him.

> As we sought to answer each question, we made it our practice to underline the real problem—the problem of sin

In addition to my daily commitment to the open-air work in the city centre, my holidays were spent involved in participation with the United Beach Missions, seeking to reach out to the holidaymakers with the gospel. My experience here inspired me to organise similar opportunities, in a number of parks around Nottingham, every Sunday during the summer months. Approximately 50 young people got involved and it was yet another great opportunity for the gospel.

During these early years I joined up with the Christian Answer team, during their Spring Bank Holiday opportunity in Speakers Corner, London. Usually there were about a hundred on the team from different parts of the country, with very able preachers, from whom one learnt a great deal in how to best communicate the gospel. More and more, I proved that, as you attempted to take the opportunities the Lord presented, so He opened up more opportunities—a lesson I was to learn over and over again. Finally, in the providence of God, I was able to enter into full time work. Initially this was with Young Life for three years and then for the next thirty years with The Open-Air Mission.

Looking back now, I have to say there were times when the going was tough. There were times of discouragement, times when I almost felt like throwing in the towel. How thankful I am for a wife who encouraged me on, and who prayed for, and with, me. How I thank the Lord for giving me strength and perseverance to endure the hard times. How I praise the Lord for those who, through the years, I have seen come to Christ as a result of hearing the gospel in the open-air. I praise Him for the increasing number of evangelists, who are now taking the good news into so many of our towns and cities.

May the Lord call yet more and more labourers into this harvest field. The need is now greater than it has ever been! May we see more and more of God's people, filled with love and compassion, going out onto the streets of our towns and cities with the greatest message that could fall on human ears. There is a vast harvest of precious souls yet to be reached.

Facing a task unfinished,
That drives us to our knees,
A need that, undiminished,
Rebukes our slothful ease,
We, who rejoice to know Thee,
Renew before Thy throne
The solemn pledge we owe Thee
To go and make Thee known.

Where other lords beside Thee
Hold their unhindered sway,
Where forces that defied Thee
Defy Thee still today,
With none to heed their crying
For life, and love, and light,
Unnumbered souls are dying,
And pass into the night.

We bear the torch that flaming
Fell from the hands of those
Who gave their lives proclaiming
That Jesus died and rose.
Ours is the same commission,
The same glad message ours,
Fired by the same ambition,
To Thee we yield our powers.

O Father who sustained them,
O Spirit who inspired,
Saviour, whose love constrained them
To toil with zeal untired,
From cowardice defend us,
From lethargy awake!
Forth on Thine errands send us
To labour for Thy sake.

Frank Houghton (1894-1972)

There's a work for Jesus, ready at your hand,
'Tis a task the Master just for you has planned.
Haste to do His bidding, yield Him service true;
There's a work for Jesus none but you can do.

> *Work for Jesus, day by day,*
> *Serve Him ever, falter never; Christ obey.*
> *Yield Him service, loyal, true:*
> *There's a work for Jesus none but you can do.*

There's a work for Jesus, humble though it be,
'Tis the very service He would ask of thee.
Go where fields are whitened, and the labourers few;
There's a work for Jesus none but you can do.

There's a work for Jesus, precious souls to bring,
Tell them of His mercies, tell them of your King.
Faint not, nor grow weary, He will strength renew;
There's a work for Jesus none but you can do.

Elsie Duncan Yale (1873-1956)